THE ORIGINS OF
WORLD WAR II

EUROPE SINCE 1500: *A Paperbound Series*

Enlightened Despotism / JOHN G. GAGLIARDO

Franco's Spain / STANLEY G PAYNE

The Third French Republic, 1870–1914 / ALEXANDER SEDGWICK

Fascist Italy / ALAN CASSELS

The Origins of World War II / KEITH EUBANK

In preparation:

Tsar Alexander I: Paternalist Reformer / ALAN MC CONNELL

The Reform Bill of 1832 / GEORGE WOODBRIDGE

Italy from Unification to 1919 / SALVATORE SALADINO

The Industrialization of Russia / WILLIAM BLACKWELL

The Russian Revolutionary Intelligentsia / PHILIP POMPER

From Versailles to Vichy: The Third French Republic, 1919–
1940 / NATHANAEL GREENE

THE ORIGINS OF
WORLD WAR II

Keith Eubank

QUEENS COLLEGE
OF THE CITY UNIVERSITY OF NEW YORK

THOMAS Y. CROWELL COMPANY

NEW YORK / ESTABLISHED 1834

For David and Ellen

Preface

This book has been written to explain the origins of the world war that began in 1939 and ended with 30,000,000 people dead and unbelievable devastation over a large part of the world. The failure to avoid this war was doubly dreadful because the outbreak of hostilities came so soon after the bloody world war that had ended in 1918. Consequently, questions about the origins of World War II and about why it could not have been prevented are extremely important. After the ordeal of 1914–1918, why had those in authority erred in assessing the threat that loomed across the Rhine? Why had there been so much reluctance to confront a once-defeated foe? Why had the aggressor been permitted to rearm? This book attempts to provide some answers to these questions.

Part of the answer, as shown in these pages, can be found in the illusion that sufficient security measures had been taken to keep the peace: war was unthinkable. But this illusion misled people into believing they were safe from world conflict until they suddenly became faced with having to choose between surrendering to the aggressor's demands or going to war again. In the past, studies of the causes of World War II have failed to give enough attention to the power of this illusion.

In the past also, historians have been quick to assign much of the responsibility for the war to the appeasers and their policies. But as I have tried to show, appeasers and appeasement are not without their merits. Although the orthodox historians have mercilessly condemned appeasement, it is important to remember that appeasement served a useful purpose. This purpose and a deep understanding of appeasement are necessary for understanding the origins of World War II. For appeasement was chosen by statesmen not out of cowardice but in response to the public's demand to avoid hostilities, if possible, forever.

The decision to postpone war until 1939 has been condemned unfairly and without full consideration of the reasons for avoiding war. It has been fashionable to denounce the democracies for their failure to go to war before 1939, when it was believed that they had a superiority over Hitler's forces. But it is important to consider that this superiority was not as obvious to the men who had the responsibility for making decisions about peace and war as it has been to historians in the years since the wars.

The British and French statesmen who led their nations into war in 1939 have also generally been denounced for their failure to conclude an alliance with the Soviet government. While charges of shortsightedness have been leveled at London and Paris for their dealings with Moscow, Soviet leaders have been acquitted of similar charges. I have tried to reassess Soviet policy (given the limited availability of Soviet documents) in view of more recent studies that show that it was not as altruistic a policy some have imagined.

The reader will realize that, although I am indebted to A. J. P. Taylor for his provocative and interesting ideas, I cannot accept his interpretation of Hitler. For in his challenge to the orthodox viewpoint, Taylor regarded Hitler as no worse in his tactics and strategy than other contemporary statesmen. Nor can I accept Taylor's argument that Hitler did not really know his mind and was simply pushed into aggression by Neville Chamberlain, and that he neither plotted nor prepared for war but rather blundered into it.

Instead, I have argued that Hitler determined his own policy according to the available opportunities and that he deliberately ran the risk of a world war for which he had not prepared Germany. But his failure to prepare ought not to be used to argue, as does Taylor, that he never intended war. For, as I have tried to show, Hitler was not averse to small wars, and he prepared Germany for such conflicts.

From the history of this period, myths have emerged about the ease of halting the militarization of the Rhineland, Stalin's eagerness to save the world from Hitler, and the wisdom of fighting over Czechoslovakia. These myths and their effects are the subject of much of this book. The influence of some of these myths has been felt in foreign policy decisions of the cold war, for these have often been made on the basis of inadequate knowledge about the origins of World War II. American statesmen have acted to halt aggression around the world on the basis of what they have imagined to be the facts about the failure to halt aggression in Europe during the 1930's. In view of this, an understanding of the cold war requires an understanding of the background of World War II.

The study of the origins of this conflict is vital for us who live under the threat of nuclear warfare, which has often been dismissed as "unthinkable" in the same manner that people between 1918 and 1939 dismissed the possibility of war as unthinkable.

These pages have profited from discussions with my students and colleagues at Queens College and at the Graduate Center of The City University of New York. I am grateful to the staff of the Paul Klapper Library of Queens College for finding out-of-print books. Stanley Duane, the general editor of the series of which this book is a part, waited patiently for a manuscript, always helpful with wise advice. James Neyland helped shape the final text; I am greatly in debt to him. The manuscript also benefited from the useful suggestions made by Professor Nathanael Greene of Wesleyan University and by Professor Hans Schmitt of New York University. However, I take full responsibility for whatever errors and shortcomings are found in these pages. As always, my wife, Marilyn Eubank, helped ease the task of writing. Without her, it would have been much harder.

Keith Eubank, *Melville, New York*

Contents

1 / "Peace," 1918–1933   1

    NOVEMBER 11, 1918   1
    THE TREATY OF VERSAILLES   2
    THE LEAGUE OF NATIONS   13
    FRENCH "SECURITY"   16
    GERMAN "GOOD FAITH"   20
    ECONOMIC CRISIS   23

2 / The Uneasy Peace, 1933–1935   25

    ADOLF HITLER   25
    REARMAMENT AND DISARMAMENT   30
    THE FOUR-POWER PACT   34
    THE DOLLFUSS AFFAIR   35
    GERMANY'S MILITARY RENAISSANCE   36
    THE FRANCO-RUSSIAN PACT   39
    THE ANGLO-GERMAN NAVAL AGREEMENT   43

3 / Years of Crisis, 1935–1938   46

    MUSSOLINI AND ETHIOPIA   46
    HITLER IN THE RHINELAND   56
    THE POPULAR FRONT AND THE SPANISH CIVIL WAR   67
    APPEASEMENT AND APPEASERS   73

4 / The Road to War, 1938   81

    THE REICHSCHANCELLERY MEETING   81
    THE ANSCHLUSS   86

CRISIS IN CZECHOSLOVAKIA 98
THE MUNICH CONFERENCE 115
THE END OF CZECHOSLOVAKIA 120

5 / WAR, 1939 130

DANZIG 130
APPEASEMENT FAILS 144
CONCLUSION 166

BIBLIOGRAPHICAL ESSAY 170

INDEX 189

1 / "Peace," 1918-1933

NOVEMBER 11, 1918

When the slaughter across Europe ceased after 11:00 AM on November 11, 1918 and peace returned to the world, the extent of the devastation that lay about the exhausted armies was new to human history. After four years of war, the piles of stones, the battered chimneys, and the roofless houses were the only signs that people had once lived in peaceful towns and villages. The trenches where men had burrowed, lived, fought, and died for a few yards of mud were mute evidence of the way of life that had destroyed the quiet countryside. The life and culture that were over had been Europe's greatest era. All that was left on the continent were the remnants of the four empires destroyed by the conflict. Over ten million people lay dead, and millions more had been wounded—but the cost in heartache and sorrow could not really be reckoned. What had begun with the murder of an Austrian archduke ended with millions of soldiers from many nations fighting across continents and oceans.

But the big losers were the countries of Europe. For Germany, the war had been a struggle for domination of world economy and trade, though the German leaders had led the German people to believe they were battling for survival against encirclement by Britain, Russia, and France. The vision of a German-dominated Europe that the German nationalists had grasped for vanished suddenly in the fall of 1918—but only after

1

they had occupied Belgium, overrun northern France, and defeated Russia.

The German government sought peace then only because it feared utter destruction and because its leaders wished to save the army and keep the nation intact. Further fighting, they reasoned, could destroy the Fatherland without bringing victory nearer. An armistice, on the other hand, could save Germany, giving the nation time to recuperate until it was better prepared to renew the effort. The German civilians, however, were not prepared for the armistice. The High Command had not informed the nation of the plight of the armies, and the German countryside was completely untouched by war. Not a foot of German territory had been lost to the enemy—how, then, could the German people reconcile defeat? They had passed through three victorious wars of unification; and in this great war, they heard nothing but optimism from the front. Defeat was unheard of, and it would not be accepted.

The Entente powers were jubilant. The dancing, cheering throngs in Piccadilly and Times Square were delirious because their great efforts were over. The rejoicing was not so delirious in Paris because too many French families were in mourning for loved ones; to the French as well as to the other victorious nations, the possibility of another world war was unthinkable. One Austrian archduke had not been worth so many dead. World war must never come again; everything must be done to avoid it.

However, twenty-one years after, the unthinkable was to happen. This second world war of the twentieth century was never really inevitable: decisions, plans, mistakes, stupidities, fears, and all the unplanned and unexpected events in human life combined to bring it about. These events have their origins in the armistice that saved German unity and the German army, prevented Allied occupation, and thus left the German people unresigned to the collapse of their dreams. The terms of the armistice were drawn deliberately to insure that Germany would be unable to renew the war. They required that German troops be withdrawn beyond the Rhine River while the Allied troops established bridgeheads on the right bank. Quantities of war materials and all of the submarine fleet were to be surrendered; sixteen capital ships were to be interned. Although Germany was to be unoccupied, the blockade would be continued.

Military occupation would have brought home to every German town the reality of defeat. But, saved by the armistice, the German army retired intact within the frontiers. Army units were welcomed back to their homeland with parades and cheering throngs, as though they were the victors instead of the vanquished. Because the army had not been routed and because German cities had escaped damage, army leaders were able to invent the myth of a "stab in the back"—the army had not been defeated on the battlefield but had been betrayed at home.

Under pressure from those in his government who wished to escape an onerous peace, Kaiser Wilhelm II had been forced to abdicate on November 9, 1918 in favor of a parliamentary monarchy. That same day, because of the outbreak of civil war and the fear of a Bolshevik uprising, the Socialist leader Philipp Scheidemann proclaimed a democratic republic. In one afternoon, Germany had adopted a form of government for which it was unprepared. Born in defeat, and shame, the Republic would be unable to avoid the stigma of the armistice, the "stab in the back," and the Treaty of Versailles, while the military leaders and the monarchy would be able to escape responsibility. The Weimar Republic—named for the city where its constitution was drafted—needed the loyalty of every German to survive, but never would all of the citizens back the strange new government with any enthusiasm. Too many people in high places were longing for the monarchy; and too many others were busy undermining the new government, even at its inception.

THE TREATY OF VERSAILLES

The delegates from twenty-seven nations assembling in Paris in January 1919 faced a host of problems. The Peace Conference's foremost concern was to prevent German domination of

Europe. There were other problems as well—many of them created by dissension among the victors themselves. Because of the enormous cost of the conflict, many were insisting that Germany pay the total cost of the war. New states had appeared, snarling over boundaries and populations; these had to be sorted out in some logical and equitable fashion. Italy was intent upon looting the remnants of the Austro-Hungarian Empire. Britain, Japan, and France insisted on dividing the German colonies among themselves. In the midst of all this, a scheme had to be devised to insure peace in the future.

The Council of Four—Woodrow Wilson of the United States, Georges Clemenceau of France, David Lloyd George of Great Britain, and Vittorio Orlando of Italy—dominated the Peace Conference. This quartet faced an enormous task—writing a peace treaty for Germany, working on treaties for the other defeated powers, restoring peace among the smaller European states, feeding the starving, establishing the League of Nations, and all the while continuing to govern their own nations. Not only did they lack the ability and temperament to accomplish their task, but each was so occupied with his own concerns that he failed to see the importance of the whole or the vital interests of the others. Wilson was chiefly interested in the League of Nations, insisting on inserting it in the treaty dealing with Germany. Orlando sought plunder for Italy, halting the conference with his demands, but Wilson forced his departure so they could get on with treaty writing. Lloyd George was concerned with insuring British naval supremacy, enlarging the empire, and reviving trade. Clemenceau was bent upon protecting France, which had been twice invaded by German armies in his lifetime.

The Treaty of Versailles was finally drafted by Wilson, Lloyd George, and Clemenceau, with limited help from the host of experts they had brought to Paris. Since 1919, the Treaty of Versailles has been severely criticized; but critics of the treaty have damned Clemenceau as the villain with Lloyd George as his accomplice, and have lauded Wilson as the White Knight who wanted to remake the world but who was thwarted by selfish European politicians. Actually, Wilson was more easily satisfied by the treaty than was Clemenceau, who, forced into compromises, warned his colleagues of the faults in the restrictions that they had placed—or had failed to place—on German might. It is true that Lloyd George achieved his aims in the treaty, but he alone attempted to improve it before Wilson left Paris. It was the White Knight who was so in favor of the treaty as it was, consenting only to minor changes, as long as he had his League of Nations.

In May 1919, the treaty terms were presented to the German delegation, which was allowed to reply in writing but not to negotiate. Living in their dream world, unconscious of the hatred accumulated during the war, the delegation was shocked by the terms presented to them. But the Weimar government had little choice other than to accept the terms. A renewal of the war, the German generals advised, could bring an end to both the German army and German unity. In the Palace of Versailles on June 28, 1919, the German delegation signed the Treaty of Versailles—but it is now evident that the German nation never intended to abide by it.

The terms of the treaty had been designed to render Germany helpless forever. The army was limited to 100,000 officers and men serving a twelve-year term of enlistment; military conscription was forbidden; the General Staff was dissolved; military schools were restricted, the manufacture of arms and munitions was curtailed, and the export and import of them were forbidden; the navy was reduced and the air force outlawed. An Allied military control commission would supervise disarmament. Germany was stripped of its colonies and was forced to cede territory to Denmark, Belgium, France, Czechoslovakia, and Poland. To give Poland an outlet to the Baltic Sea, East Prussia was detached by a strip of land that became known as the Polish Corridor, an area that included Danzig, which would be a free city under League of Nations administration. To insure compliance with the treaty terms, the Rhineland would be occupied by Allied troops for fifteen years. France would rule the Saar for fifteen years, after which final control would be determined by a plebiscite.

Article 231, erroneously labeled "the war guilt clause," which introduced the reparations section of the treaty, was incomprehensible to the German populace. It required that the defeated accept the "responsibility of Germany and her allies for causing all the loss and damage which the allies suffered as a result of the war imposed upon them by the aggression of Germany and her allies." The Weimar Republic assigned the task of refuting war guilt to a special office set up in the Foreign Ministry. This office subsidized books—suppressing some—and hired journalists and historians to convince the world of German innocence. The treaty also required that Germany pay for reparations; but because the Council of Four could not agree on an amount, it had to be determined later by a special commission. This seemed to German patriots to be a "blank check" designed to ruin Germany forever; they were unwilling to conceive of a means whereby Germany would be able to provide the reparations. Unemployed army officers, university professors, civil servants, and even clergymen swelled the chorus damning the treaty and the new republic that had accepted it. Rather conveniently, they forgot that they themselves had set the precedent for this kind of "war guilt" in the Treaty of Brest-Litovsk, when they had detached Russian land (a deed remembered well by Wilson). They ignored the heavy indemnity Bismarck had demanded of France in 1871 and the seizure of Alsace-Lorraine. Most important, they failed to consider that, had they won in 1918, the defeated Allies would have suffered heavier reparations and greater loss of land than they themselves were suffering.

With the Treaty of Versailles, the Allies imagined they had found a means for preventing German domination of Europe;

but the treaty was deceiving—its strength was an illusion. It was not harsh enough to render Germany impotent forever, but it was severe enough to provide German nationalists with a cause they could use to rally the nation against the treaty. British and American delegations had not hesitated to impose heavy obligations on Germany, but neither was willing to insist on a means to compel fulfillment of the terms. Both condemned French efforts to insure German compliance. The French wanted the Treaty of Versailles to be a safeguard against German aggression; but Wilson and Lloyd George assumed that Germany would willingly enforce the provisions, acting as its own policeman. Thanks to the Anglo-American objections, only the Rhineland would be occupied, and it was to be evacuated within fifteen years. Penalties for German violations of treaty terms were non-existent. When the occupation of the Rhineland ended in 1930 and Allied troops withdrew, nothing remained within Germany to guarantee German observance of the treaty terms. Germany was able to rearm and to reoccupy the Rhineland.

This is not to say that the Allies completely ignored the problem of policing German disarmament. It is simply that their policing was never permitted to become effective. The treaty set up the Allied Control Commission to ensure German compliance, but its unarmed control officers encountered a well-organized attempt to frustrate their efforts. Using passive resistance, insults, and physical intimidation, the German army systematically blocked the Commission. To complicate matters further, the British control officers received minimal support from London. In 1927, at German insistence, the Allied Control Commission was withdrawn, and its final report on violations of disarmament provisions was suppressed.

The Reparations Commission set up by the treaty finally presented a bill to Germany for $33,000,000,000, in gold. France needed reparations to pay its heavy reconstruction costs and the debts owed to Britain and the United States. Britain refused cancellation of debts owed by France unless the United States was willing to cancel British debts. But the United States was unwilling to cancel any debts whatsoever.

It is evident now that Germany never intended to pay the entire amount. The Weimar government requested a scaling down of payment and a new assessment of German ability to pay. The French rejected this flatly, arguing that, if neither London nor Washington considered French ability to pay, this yardstick should not be applied to Germany. An international conference to work out a new settlement might have been able to solve the muddle, but the United States refused to negotiate, out of fear that the French and British might succeed in lowering their debts. But blame cannot be placed fully upon the United States nor upon the Allies in general. Certainly their failure to come to an agreement on reduction of reparations left Germany faced with the necessity of paying the full amount; but Germany was not so much weakened economically by the reparations as angered by them. What Germany ultimately paid in reparations proved to be less than France had paid after the Franco-Prussian War.

Only one military attempt was made to enforce the reparations section of the treaty, and that attempt failed. France and Belgium, concluding that Germany had defaulted in reparations payment, sent troops to occupy the Ruhr on January 11, 1923. The governments in Brussels and Paris were under the illusion that German workers could be compelled to labor for the victors. What they found was the contrary: workers in the Ruhr, urged on by the German government, struck and sabotaged their efforts. In an attempt to support the resistance, the German government increased the printing of money, with the result that the German economy, unstable since the war, suffered a disastrous inflation. Where, before the war, the mark was valued at four to the dollar, by August 1923, it had been devalued to 4,600,000 to the dollar. Many people resorted to barter, while those who lived on fixed incomes were wiped out. Wages had such little buying power that the average workingman was hard put to purchase the barest necessities, while shrewd manipulators took advantage of the inflation to build up fortunes, and German industrialists paid off their indebtedness in worthless marks.

Eventually, the French and Belgian governments found occupation costs more than they were able to collect in reparations. In addition, they were faced with the disapproval of the United States and British governments. Fearing the German financial problem would spread, they began an investigation into the problems of reparations. The result was the plan presented by the Dawes Commission, which proposed that reparations payments should be based on Germany's ability to pay, with that ability to be determined by an "index of prosperity." But the Dawes Plan did not stop there. It proposed international loans to help the German economy recover. France and Belgium accepted the plan in 1925 and withdrew their troops. Loans, chiefly from the United States, poured into Germany, creating prosperity for the defeated country, although "victorious" Britain and France, who also owed war debts, were not permitted a similar advantage. With the United States loans, German industry was able to expand its war-making potential far beyond that of France and Britain.

Germany had managed to pull victory from defeat. After this, it would not be faced with French attempts to enforce the Versailles treaty alone. In addition, as if being rewarded for resistance, German industry was being heaped with financial aid from former enemies. Here, only five years after the close of war, the pattern was being set for what was to come. Germany was expressing dissatisfaction with the treaty it had "accepted," and the victors were making concessions that eventually would prove too liberal. They instituted the policy of appeasement that they later would curse bitterly.

In condemning French occupation of the Ruhr, the United States and Britain had pointed to the Treaty of Versailles, reasoning that this kind of action had not been provided for. But these would-be arbiters of international morality had little right to point. During the peace conference, Wilson and Lloyd George had signed mutual defense treaties with Clemenceau, guaranteeing aid to France in the event of German invasion. This guarantee was to last until the League of Nations had sufficient strength to impose peace, at which time France would have both the treaty and the League as bulwarks against German aggression. However, these agreements were not a part of Wilson's plans for Europe; they were simply temporary expedients he was willing to accept in order to circumvent Clemenceau's demands for detachment of the Rhineland. Neither he nor Lloyd George ever intended that the guarantee should become a permanent military alliance. The United States Senate only reinforced this intent when it refused even to consider the agreement after it had rejected the Treaty of Versailles. With Wilson's signature not worth the paper it was written on, Britain was not about to be bound by the guarantee.

Thus, deserted by its allies, France was left with only the League of Nations to protect its security, and that was cold comfort at best. France would be able to achieve security only by forcing Germany to adhere to the provisions of the Versailles treaty, but the devastated country could not accomplish alone a task that eventually would require the combined efforts of Britain, the United States, and Soviet Russia. Try as he might, Clemenceau would not be able to convince a distrustful Britain or an isolationist United States of the rightness of his cause. And certainly, France could not turn to Russia, which—enmeshed in its own internal problems and resentful of a peace settlement that excluded it—felt more sympathy for Germany than for France.

As a result, the treaty satisfied no one. Certainly, with the treaty rejected by the Senate, United States dissatisfaction was apparent. But the British critics had been outspoken against the treaty provisions even before the treaty was signed. They considered it a dictated peace, based on military power, and believed its "idealism" to be nothing more than hypocrisy. Self-determination, they pointed out, had been denied Germans in Austria and Czechoslovakia; the treaty spoke of territorial integrity, but Germany had been robbed of its own lands; and, most important to many of the critics, the enormous reparations would bar a return to prosperity. John Maynard Keynes denounced the reparations in one of the strongest assaults—and the most successful. In *Economic Consequences of the Peace,* he claimed that the treaty was incompatible with overall European economic prosperity because it wrecked the German economy. If Europe were to recover, Germany had to recover; and this Germany could not do unless the treaty were revised. Keynes's arguments lent valuable assistance to the case for German appeasement, sustaining the plea that, because Germany had been so mistreated, it should be unilaterally allowed to revise the treaty.

During the 1920s and 1930s, it was in fashion to damn the treaty, but the criticisms were really unfair. After all, Germany had legally accepted the treaty, and Germany was unoccupied except for the Rhineland. And even that was to be evacuated before the expiration of the fifteen-year period set down in the treaty. The reparations Germany had to pay were high, but they were proportionately no heavier than those imposed on France in 1871, and France then had not received loans to speed its recovery. France had paid the reparations in order to be rid of an unwanted occupation army. There is no doubt that Germany could have paid the reparations had the nation been so inclined, and it actually would have been to its advantage. The industrial expansion resulting from endeavors to make payments would have given Germany economic hegemony in Europe.

Although the loss of its colonies wounded Germany's pride, there was no real damage. In fact, the German taxpayers should have rejoiced at getting rid of an unnecessary luxury. Once Germany had suffered defeat, the loss of Alsace-Lorraine was inevitable, but that was the only German territory given to France. Nor were the lands ceded to Belgium, Czechoslovakia, and Denmark crippling losses; and Poland had as much right to be an independent nation as Germany had. It is true that the separation of East Prussia from the rest of Germany caused by the creation of the Polish Corridor was not a natural geographical distinction, but it was not as vast a separation as that of Alaska from the United States. In terms of potential, the losses that Germany suffered were not as heavy as those imposed on Russia in the Treaty of Brest-Litovsk, when Germany had taken 54 percent of Russian industry and 34 percent of the Russian population.

Thus, the Treaty of Versailles, contrary to the beliefs of early critics, left Germany's potential strength virtually untouched. In manpower, resources, and size, Germany was still the largest nation in Europe, except for Russia. And the war had not turned its land into wasteland as it had with French and Belgian land. It was in an ideal position, for the collapse of the Habsburg empire, the defeat of imperial Germany, and the Bolshevik victory in Russia created a power vacuum in eastern Europe; and the only nation in a position to fill that vacuum was Germany. The fledgling nations that stretched from the Baltic to the Mediterranean—with their oil, factories, farms, and natural resources —beckoned to the strongest bidder. Fashioned under the terms of the Treaty of Versailles, the German army was a long-term professional force, and it was the largest and most efficient in Central Europe. None of Germany's neighbors could afford so large a professional army—especially not France, whose forces were made up of conscripts led by antiquated generals.

Thus, the Treaty of Versailles deserved criticism, but the criticism it received was not the criticism it deserved. Even if the treaty had been amended in line with its criticisms, the events that were to take place in the ensuing two decades could not have been avoided.

THE LEAGUE OF NATIONS

Imbedded in the Treaty of Versailles was the Covenant of the League of Nations, dear to the heart of Woodrow Wilson. It had been placed there at his insistence. According to the Covenant, the League of Nations guaranteed the territorial integrity and independence of all its members, but it did not stipulate how it would carry out its guarantee. It simply indicated that it would consider the act of any League member declaring war without completing the proscribed procedures for settling disputes as an act of war against the entire League of Nations. In the event of such an occurrence, League members were to impose economic and financial sanctions immediately. They were in no way obliged to make war on the aggressor or to contribute to armed forces that would enforce the League Covenant. The League Council could, however, "recommend" that its members contribute to such a force. This was complicated by the fact that, because all decisions of the Council had to be unanimous, swift action was absolutely impossible. In the event of Council failure to reach unanimous agreement on a means for ending a dispute, the League's members were to be free to take whatever action they deemed wise. This, of course, included the freedom to do nothing.

The League has been consistently blamed for the failure to prevent the outbreak of World War II. These charges generally have been unjust. The League of Nations was not intended as a military alliance, prepared to rush ships and troops to protect a nation from aggression. The statesmen who drafted the Covenant believed that World War I could have been avoided if the great powers had possessed some means for delaying hostilities while they instituted negotiations to settle the disputes. They designed the League of Nations as a mechanism to delay the rush of nations into conflict, not to protect the victim from aggression by an alliance. There had been attempts to devise a military alliance, but these had been quashed by Wilson, who was a proponent of the theory that it was a confrontation between alliances that had started the war.

Thus, the League of Nations, like the Treaty of Versailles, created a false sense of security because many people imagined that it was poised, ready to move swiftly to punish the aggressor and enforce the peace; but, thanks to the conservatism of its creators and the power of nationalism, the League of Nations would not be equipped to handle the arduous labors that would be thrust upon it during its brief history. Idealists imagined that the League would be the supreme arbiter of international affairs, but the great powers who dominated the League would not permit it to handle matters vital to their national interests. They were willing to use the League when it suited them —when the disputes were minor affairs involving less powerful nations. But they were unwilling to give up a certain degree of their power in order to give the organization any real power of its own. Especially after the international crises broke out across Europe in the 1930s, the major powers were unwilling to make changes in the Covenant that would give the League sufficient strength to halt aggression.

The League experienced its first crisis involving a major power in 1923, when Benito Mussolini, the new Italian dictator, demanded indemnity for the Italian commission murdered while involved in delimiting the frontiers between Greece and Albania. Because the Greek government had rejected his exorbitant demands, Mussolini ordered the bombardment and occupation of Corfu. The League was at a loss for a way to resolve the situation. Deprived of the leadership of the great powers, particularly France and Great Britain, there was little the League could do. Britain would not press the Greek case for fear Italy would walk out of the League; and France could not be bothered with using the League against any country other than Germany. Because neither power would support the Greek appeal, the matter was shunted to a conference of ambassadors, which awarded Mussolini his indemnity, thereby enhancing the dictator's reputation for pugnacity and establishing a precedent for avoiding direct confrontation with Fascist aggression.

Perhaps the best illustration of the weakness purposely built into the League of Nations was the Manchurian crisis. In September 1931, alleging that Japanese interests were endangered, Japanese troops began a "police action" in Manchuria, resulting in the setting up of the puppet state of Manchukuo. In 1933, after the League of Nations adopted the report of the Lytton Commission condemning Japanese actions, Japan withdrew from the League. The recommendations of the Lytton Commission were notably fair and sensible—Manchuria should be administered by an autonomous government with ultimate sovereignty under China, but with international police to guarantee protection of Japanese interests. But, when Japan refused to abide by the solution, the League could do nothing more than refuse recognition to the stamps, money, and passports of the puppet state.

The only means available to enforce Japanese adherence to these recommendations were in the hands of the major powers, and they were only lukewarm in their support of the League action. While they did not want to sanction Japanese aggression, their own interests prevented them from actively supporting the League's resolution. Britain's new coalition government, though headed by Labor pacifist J. Ramsay MacDonald, was dominated by Tories, who preferred Japan to China because Japan was an old ally and would be more likely to defend British interests in Manchuria. Furthermore, the MacDonald government was too busy trying to avert national bankruptcy to be greatly concerned with events in the Far East. France could not be bothered because Japan was no threat to French borders; and the United States, still influenced by isolationism and not wishing to be overcommitted outside its borders, barely managed a pronouncement of "non-recognition."

Though the Manchurian crisis was a second wound to the

League of Nations, it was less a failure of the League than a failure of the countries responsible for the formation of the League. They had built the slow, inefficient, and cumbersome mechanism into the League Covenant, and they had failed to stand by the League in a moment of crisis. The only attempt to resolve this weakness occurred in 1932, when France attempted to have troops set aside in constant readiness at the disposal of the League; but, because this smacked of a superstate, Britain killed the proposal.

The weakness most often pointed out is that of United States' failure to join the League. This has created the myth that American participation somehow would have strengthened the League and managed to stave off war. Actually, if the United States had taken an active role in the League, history would have been changed very little. United States participation would not have altered the basic weaknesses in the League's procedures. Even with the United States, these procedures would have remained to foster aggression. After all, a United States president had written these weaknesses into the League's Covenant. The only thing the United States could have done to maintain peace would have been to have stationed American troops permanently in western Europe; but the average voter, congressman, and senator in the United States recoiled at such a thought. It would require a Pearl Harbor—an attack directly involving United States interests—for an American president to be able to commit American troops to the preservation of world peace.

FRENCH "SECURITY"

Until Hitler came to power, Europe was living in a fantasy world, wrapped up in the illusion that a conflict like the last could never be repeated because Germany had reformed and because the newly formed League would guard the peace. Only a madman would be willing to court another bloodbath to achieve power, and madmen could not become heads of governments. The only one of the Versailles powers to doubt the fantasy and to search for a greater security was France, which, finding security neither in the treaty nor in the League, immediately began to cast about for alliances.

France would have preferred the old alliance with Russia, but the Bolshevik revolution in Russia and the fear of a similar take-over at home forced France to turn to nations that were weak, disunited, and quarrelsome. The first steps in developing an alliance were an agreement with Belgium in 1920 and one with Poland in 1921. Both promised mutual aid in case of German aggression or German mobilization, or in case of any need to enforce the Versailles treaty. In 1924, France allied with Czechoslovakia to oppose restoration of the Habsburg and Hohenzollern monarchies. The French alliance system was completed by an agreement with Rumania in 1926 and one with Yugoslavia in 1927. France also sought to negotiate a pact with the British, but Britain was fearful of the old problem of competing alliances and the new problem of French domination of Europe.

Despite the external appearances, this latter fear had little basis for existence. The main cause for it was the French relationship to the countries of eastern Europe. Britain considered the Little Entente as being nothing more than a French puppet. However, this alliance—formed in 1920–1921 by Czechoslovakia, Yugoslavia, and Rumania as a protection against Hungary— was connected to France only insofar as France had its individual pacts with each of them. It was certainly nothing on the order of what Britain suspected it of being.

Furthermore, beneath the illusion of these alliances, there was little real strength. Each of these new nations was plagued with minority problems. Self-determination was proving easier to preach than to practice, and boundaries drawn up at the conference table were proving to be less distinct than the peacemakers believed.

In giving Posen and Polish Pomerania (the Polish Corridor)

to Poland, the Versailles powers had given Poland a German minority as well. In 1921, after a short war with Russia, Poland gained territory from the Ukraine and White Russia that would reinstate the boundaries of 1772, but it also gave Poland a Russian minority consisting of 4½ million Ukrainians and 1½ million White Russians. As long as Poland had these minorities, good relations with Germany and Russia would be difficult if not impossible.

Poland was certainly not the ideal ally for an insecure France. To be of any assistance, Poland had to be strong; and, to gain strength, it was necessary to antagonize either Germany or Soviet Russia or both. As long as Germany suffered from the war and Russia labored to recover from its revolution, Poland could pretend to be a great power; but, because of a shortage of manpower and poor industrial potential, Poland would not be able to achieve its dream before Germany and Russia would be able to reclaim their old power. Then, the minorities Poland had acquired would prove to be a disadvantage—indeed, they would be a threat to Polish independence. It is true the appearance was that of an advantage to France: Germany was faced with France on the west and Poland on the east. But France did not consider the possibility of a threat to Poland's own eastern border. Poland would never be able to engage all its forces against Germany as long as there was the threat of Russia to the east.

The other major ally of France—Czechoslovakia—was also strategically vulnerable. The new country was narrow and entirely cut off from the sea, surrounded by Germany, Austria, Hungary, Rumania, and Poland. And, like Poland, the Treaty of Versailles had given Czechoslovakia the problem of minorities with loyalties outside the proscribed borders. The Magyars in Slovakia beckoned to Hungary. The Sudeten Germans of Bohemia despised the Czechs and longed to be returned to Germany. To complicate this problem further, the fledgling nation snatched Teschen from Poland while the Poles had their backs turned trying to gain territory from Russia.

France's other allies—Rumania and Yugoslavia—had been similarly handicapped. The borders set down by the peacemakers for Rumania were disputed by Hungary, Bulgaria, and Russia, while those for Yugoslavia were challenged by Italy, Bulgaria, and Hungary. The peacemakers' attempts had been laudable; had the boundary problems been as clear-cut as they had envisioned, the result of their attempts might have been equally as laudable. As it was, they had created as many problems as they had solved.

By turning to these new nations—with their new problems —for alliances, France was creating more of a problem than it was solving. These allies had too many enemies—both foreign and domestic—to contribute much to the defense of France, but they all expected French troops to be ready to protect them. The system of alliances proved to be a misalliance, economically as well as militarily. Ideally, the French economy should have been a complement to the economies of its allies, but its problems and those of its allies were identical. France had agricultural surpluses, and so did its allies. What French allies needed were industrial goods, but French industry was barely adequate for French needs. As a result, the countries of eastern Europe turned to the only European power who could supply the industrial goods—Germany. It also proved to be Germany who would become the market for their surpluses in agricultural produce, oil, and raw materials.

To complete the insurance against German attack, France erected the Maginot Line. Stretching across northeastern France, it would protect Alsace-Lorraine with a series of interlocking concrete and steel fortresses with underground command posts, barracks, storerooms, kitchens, ammunition dumps, and powerhouses in each. An underground railroad would connect them. The planning behind this was indicative of the policy of the French General Staff, a policy based on the concept that a good defense is far better than a good offense. In the final test, the Maginot Line—like all the other guarantees—would not provide France with the security it needed.

GERMAN "GOOD FAITH"

With the Locarno Conference, the French security system suffered a deadly blow. Due primarily to the efforts of the German Foreign Minister, Gustav Stresemann, Germany managed to remove a large part of the restrictions of the Versailles treaty. Stresemann, like other patriotic Germans, hated the treaty, but he saw that a continuation of open opposition would not restore Germany to its old position of power in Europe. He endeavored instead to subvert the treaty restrictions by evidencing German "good faith," an attitude intended to show that the new German government was as dedicated to the peace as were Germany's former enemies.

Stresemann's purpose was to rid Germany of the occupation troops in the Rhineland and to avoid a second Franco-Belgian occupation of the Ruhr. In January 1925, Stresemann queried the British government on the possibilities of the demilitarization of the Rhineland if Germany were willing to sign an agreement recognizing the present French–German boundaries. This would have been a German acknowledgment of French rights to Alsace-Lorraine, but the Allies were doubtful about the wisdom of making such an agreement. They were unwilling to withdraw from the Rhineland until they were certain that Germany had complied with the disarmament provisions of the Versailles treaty. Faced with distrust—if not opposition—from the military and the right-wing segments of his government, Stresemann hoped to be able to dissociate the disarmament question from any international negotiations. By succeeding in this, he achieved Germany's first major victory against the Versailles treaty.

The treaties signed at Locarno on October 16, 1925 said

nothing about German disarmament. In effect these treaties gave much to Germany and required nothing of it. It is true, of course, Germany was giving up any right to Alsace-Lorraine and guaranteeing the *status quo* of its western borders with France and Belgium; but the German government would not guarantee the eastern borders of Germany, because it intended to attempt to regain territory that had been given to Poland. All the signators guaranteed the demilitarized zone of Germany; and France, Belgium, and Germany—with Britain and Italy signing as guarantors—renounced the use of war except in fulfillment of the obligations of the Covenant of the League of Nations or in self-defense. A violation of the guarantees by one of the signatories obligated the others to aid the aggrieved party. Treaties of arbitration were signed, as well as treaties of mutual assistance between France and Czechoslovakia and France and Poland. Stresemann was sacrificing nothing that was German— he knew the military was not equipped for an invasion of France—and he had indirectly acquired acknowledgment of German integrity, a left-handed blow to the Treaty of Versailles.

Because France had been unable to obtain a guarantee of Germany's eastern borders, the guarantee of the western border meant nothing. In effect, the treaties of Locarno meant that Germany was free to do as it wished in Poland and Czechoslovakia, to whom France was committed; but, if France attempted to fulfill its commitments to these countries, it would be breaking a Locarno agreement. The only concession Stresemann made in eastern Europe was to accept arbitration treaties with Poland and Czechoslovakia, but he refused a guarantee for these treaties.

The road had been paved for the end of occupation in the Rhineland. Germany was making a display of its good intentions. Because Germany had mended its ways, it was implied, the Allies should reciprocate by relaxing the treaty. Since Germany had guaranteed its frontiers, it would be appropriate for the Allies to withdraw troops from the Rhineland. Stresemann and

Germany were chipping away at the restrictions, to the effect that by 1930—five years ahead of the proscribed time—the Rhineland was no longer occupied.

The Allies had committed a grave mistake. Evacuation would not succeed in appeasing Germany for long. Had the occupation forces remained there until 1935, as the Versailles treaty had planned, the Nazi threat might have been averted. By that time the threat was so obvious that France and Britain probably would have kept their troops in the Rhineland until the danger passed. As it was, they gave in to a brief period of German good faith, thus losing their right to intervene when the danger had returned. Having thrown away their strategic advantage, the Allies received no thanks from Germany. Instead, they were met with more demands for concessions.

Again, the mistake had been made despite French protests. Aside from Germany, the country most pleased with the results of the Locarno Conference was Britain, which accepted the pledges precisely because they were worthless. If the treaties of Locarno had committed Britain to a war in eastern Europe or if they had required a military alliance in western Europe, Britain would not have agreed to them. The vagueness of five nations allied against "aggression," but not against an aggressor, delighted the British government. Besides the promises in eastern Europe, France had wanted a promise of immediate aid in case of aggression; but Britain would allow no such thing.

Germany played upon the lack of commitment among the Allies. By 1926, it had gained admission to the League of Nations; and, by 1927, with Stresemann's guidance, it managed to achieve the end of the Allied Control Commission and to have the Commission's final report suppressed. German "good faith" was achieving the desired results. By creating the illusion of peace while secretly rebuilding its army, Germany was on the way toward its goal of tearing up the Versailles treaty.

To complete the illusion of peace, negotiations were instituted in 1928 that led to the Kellogg–Briand Pact, renouncing war as a means for resolving disputes and pledging peaceful settlement of all agreements. Starting as a Franco-American agreement, this pact that was to outlaw war for all time would eventually be signed by sixty-five nations, including the Soviet Union. Who could find fault with so noble a principle? The signing and ratification by so many nations bore witness to the power of the illusion that another world war was impossible. The problem with this peace effort—as with others in this period—was that the peacemakers' blind optimism failed to consider a means for enforcing the peace in case one of the members broke the faith, as indeed one would do.

ECONOMIC CRISIS

The optimism of the peace—both in Europe and in the United States—was marred at this time by economic failures. The American stock market crash in 1929 was an indication of the dangers ahead for Europe. Immediately, it had the effect of a forced recall of loans made to Austria and Germany. It had been these loans, effected under the Dawes Plan, that had made possible the resurgence of the German economy. Now their withdrawal had the opposite effect. In 1930, the money market of Central Europe was gradually tightened, forcing industry to restrict production. In May 1931, the collapse of the Kreditanstalt set off a series of bank failures throughout Central Europe. The resulting fall in production and prices brought widespread unemployment, with all of Europe suffering.

Ignorant of the subtleties of economics, the conservative European financiers argued that the depression could be ended only by balancing budgets, cutting government expenditures, and lowering taxes—all of which they proceeded to do, thereby making things worse. Requests from the military for armaments consistently encountered the argument that manufacturing useless weapons would call for increased taxes, and increasing taxes would prolong the depression. In Britain during these years, it became standard procedure to lower military budgets annually. However, whether from economic foresight or from military persistence, Germany managed to find the means to increase military expenditures, thereby rebuilding the army and keeping some people employed.

The unemployed were crying out for action from their various governments, thus lending encouragement to economic nationalism and frequently resulting in leaders adopting irresponsible measures that were harmful to other nations. While Franklin Roosevelt's domestic program had its benefits, his foreign policy had disastrous results. In 1933, the major powers met in London to attempt to reach an agreement on stabilizing international currency exchange. But Roosevelt personally destroyed their hopes by refusing to accept any agreement they might make and by insisting on maintaining his isolationist monetary policy. This is not to say that, if he had agreed to negotiate, Europe's economic problems would have been solved, but it would have left the door open for some sort of economic cooperation on an international level. By being unwilling to face this struggle, Roosevelt unknowingly was increasing the possibilities for a greater struggle later on. Left to their own devices, the countries of Europe grasped at whatever straws looked promising.

In Germany, the more than six million unemployed grasped for any promise of an active program to replace the confusion of the Weimar Republic. This proved to be a boon to the rising Adolf Hitler. The political fortunes of this man, who otherwise might have been nothing more than a troublesome rabble-rouser, thrived on the depression. For a country accustomed to strong leadership, the confusion of the more moderate leaders seemed fearful. The German people looked Left and Right, seeking strength in extremes. When membership in the Communist party rose, many a good German citizen saw in Hitler the only bulwark against bolshevism. The disappointment, uncertainty, and fear of the time left the German people open for the endeavors of a demagogue.

2 / The Uneasy Peace, 1933-1935

ADOLF HITLER

Adolf Hitler was the shiftless son of an Austrian customs official. A lazy student whose grades were generally either poor or failing, he never completed his schooling. Though he had once tried to gain admittance to the Vienna Art Academy, he was totally unprepared for any profession or trade. He was incapable of holding a steady job, and he had to exist on an allowance from his father's estate, enhanced by cheating his sister and mother out of their share. All things considered, he was a most unlikely candidate for the savior of Germany.

At the outbreak of World War I, young Adolf had enlisted in the Bavarian army. Army life not only supplied him with financial security and comradeship, but it also faced him with what he considered a profound experience: war, he found, was not hideous, but heroic and glorious; it had given his life a meaning. During the war, he had been wounded, had been promoted to corporal, and had been twice decorated with the Iron Cross. After the war, he was not likely to let this moment of glory pass.

Serving as a political agent for the army, Hitler was instructed to investigate the German Workers' Party in Munich. While involved in his investigation, he became interested in the activities of this little group and accepted their invitation to join.

It was not long before he controlled the organization. Because there were only about forty members, he had no trouble in dominating the party and exploiting it for his own personal power. The new leader built the membership, broadened the party's program, and changed its name to the National Socialist German Workers' Party, soon to become known to history as the Nazis.

It was only after he had begun serving the party that Hitler fully developed his talents as a demagogue. He spoke on Munich street corners, from the platforms of great auditoriums, and in smoke-filled Munich beer halls, denouncing the Versailles treaty, the Bolsheviks, and the Jews as the reasons for Germany's problems. For him, the spoken word was becoming a weapon that he could use with masterly skill to bring the German masses under his spell.

The German people did not want to hear dull statistics or long-winded political platitudes. They wanted to be absolved from the guilt of 1918 and from the disgrace of the Versailles treaty. They wanted someone to soothe their fears of inflation and depression. When Hitler stepped on the platform in a great auditorium, he was able to grasp this and give them what they wanted—impassioned oratory that would obliterate all common sense and give them something they could believe in so strongly that they would be willing to die for it. He gave them the image of a dynamic, authoritarian leader who would rescue Germany from disgrace and return it to a position of dominance in Europe.

Although Hitler must personally bear the greatest burden of guilt for World War II, he could never have come to power had World War I not made German values so unnatural. Certainly, he could never have attained power under the Hohenzollerns. The German system of values was inverted still further by an exaggerated fear that the Bolshevik revolution in Russia might be repeated in Germany. The Nazis pointed to the Communist minority—small and ineffective, but Communist nevertheless— that had managed to find its way into the Reichstag. They provided Hitler with another target to add to his favorite—the Weimar Republic.

In conservative Bavaria, in November 1923, Hitler led the Beer Hall *Putsch,* in an attempt to seize control of the Bavarian government as the first step in overthrowing the Weimar government. However, his supporters deserted him, and the *Putsch* failed. The future Fuehrer was given a five-year jail sentence, but he was pardoned after serving only one year. Though the *Putsch* in 1923 was itself a failure, it served to give Hitler a national reputation that he could build upon. To take advantage of this reputation, he began writing a book while in prison. The result —*Mein Kampf*—failed in its goal; instead of attracting further attention to him, the book would not become popular until after Hitler himself achieved national prominence. Many have considered *Mein Kampf* to be a carefully contrived program for world conquest, but it is most unlikely that the book was intended as anything of the sort. In fact, what Hitler's publisher had hoped for was a personal record of the struggles of the little band of Nazis. What Hitler gave him was simply a rambling collection of threats, denunciations, and cries for vengeance from a minor German politician who then seemed to have little chance of obtaining political office.

What Hitler presented to his receptive audience, both in his book and in his speeches, was not a plan for conquest but a set of goals for Germany. *Lebensraum,* or "living space," was needed if Germany was to have sufficient population, food, and natural resources to dominate Europe. This required control of territory in Central Europe and in Russia. It required union of the German peoples, who were now divided among several countries. The need for the destruction of France—and later of England— came from their existence as barriers to German domination of Europe. Certainly, in the early years, Hitler did not have a master plan to conquer the world through world war.

Rather, Hitler was an opportunist, ready to seize any chance to achieve his goals. In accomplishing what he did, he was aided by his patience and his masterful sense of timing. In the power vacuum of Central Europe, Hitler found his greatest opportunity, one that had been built for him by the defects in the Treaty of Versailles. Between Germany and Russia lay a collection of small states that were weak, quarrelsome, deficient in manpower and industry; and none of them had an army approximating that permitted Germany by the treaty. To cap it off, each of these countries possessed minorities that could be exploited as German.

It is rare that an opportunist has had the wealth of opportunities that were presented to Hitler. In the beginning, when he first started to take control of the Nazi organization and build its membership, he saw confused young men coming out of the trenches, disgusted with the defeat, despairing at economic difficulties, and searching for someone—anyone—to blame for the misfortunes they were unable to understand. A better opportunity could not have been set up for a right-wing demagogue. Even something as unlikely as the advent of the airplane was an opportunity just waiting for the rising politician. By using the airplane in conducting his political campaigns, he was able to make himself known in every important German city and town, taking his carefully staged rallies to the masses. Though he lost the presidential election of 1932, he managed through his whirlwind campaign to make himself and his ideas known all over Germany.

Possibly the strangest of his opportunities came to him in the form of Joseph Stalin. Whether it was because he was still new to international affairs or because he was misinformed, it is hard to say; but whatever the reason, the usually clever Stalin erred in his assessment of nazism as fully as did the bourgeois capitalist statesmen. What Stalin saw in Germany in 1930 was a parliamentary government headed for collapse because neither a single party nor a coalition could achieve a majority. Because he considered the Social Democrats—the leading party in the foundation of the Weimar Republic—to be seducing German workers from the Marxist faith, he was easily misled in appraising the Nazis. Stalin saw them as the natural Fascist prelude to the inevitable Communist revolution, and he allowed German Communists to cooperate with the Fascists in smashing the Social Democrats and disrupting the Weimar Republic. Had Hitler been an ordinary politician, Stalin's plans might have succeeded; but Stalin had not reckoned with an inspired demagogue.

The western statesmen, however, were so befuddled at being faced with a man unlike anyone they had ever had to deal with that they hurried to order the objects of Hitler's wrath to surrender lest he launch a war. This former inhabitant of the Vienna gutters and the Munich slums, who had survived by learning the intricacies of hitting below the belt and stabbing in the back, had the advantage over the kind of men who knew only the standards of Whitehall and the Quai d'Orsay.

Hitler was seldom troubled by the unfavorable opinions of experts and professional diplomats, and he did not shrink from policies frightening to those with traditional attitudes on international affairs. Knowing that average men recoiled at the thought of a repetition of the kind of slaughter that occurred at Verdun, Hitler threatened it to frighten his opponents into concessions. After the fact, some historians have argued that Hitler's threats were bluffs, but the events of September 1939 prove that he was quite prepared to carry out his threats. Perhaps it was because they never had the responsibility for calling a bluff with empty hands that these men can attribute a bluff to Hitler in 1938.[1]

The men helping Hitler made up one of the most curious phenomena of the time. The curiosity is not how few men opposed Hitler but how many men served him gladly—intelligent men who cheered his speeches, obeyed his laws, and ultimately died for him in the Russian snows and the Berlin rubble.

[1] Cf. A.J.P. Taylor, *The Origins of the Second World War* (London, 1961), p. 167.

Few dared question the goals that Hitler revealed in his statements to German officials, in his speeches to the nation, and in *Mein Kampf*. Who knows how many Germans understood his goals fully, but did not flinch from carrying out his orders despite the cost? Professional diplomats, generals and admirals, industrialists, civil servants—all carried out their duties as loyal German citizens, with only an occasional complaint *sotto voce*.

Perhaps each of them, caught up in his own immediate situation, believed he was responding as well as he could. Certainly, there were members of the High Command—some of the older officers—who were disgusted by Hitler's tactics, but who hoped they could tame him in order to use his Nazi party to provide mass support for the army's expansion efforts. These were men who foolishly believed that Hitler's goals coincided with theirs, the only difference being that he craved them more speedily. The only goal for them was the rebuilding of the army and thereby regaining the German stronghold in Europe. If Hitler could help them to achieve this end, they would make allowances for any minor disagreements they might have.

Since Hitler had been proclaiming his purposes while welding Germany into a mighty war machine, why was there no one who would halt him before he conquered most of Europe? The answer is that there was no one who wanted to stop him. He seemed either to be an unpleasant nightmare that would swiftly vanish if everyone talked loudly enough about collective security or to be a politician who delivered bombastic speeches solely for German consumption. Hitler could never have been checked without a war ultimately involving most of Europe. At that price, no one cared to stop him. Until Hitler actually started the war, every nation shrank from checking him for fear that they might bring on a conflagration like the last.

REARMAMENT AND DISARMAMENT

When Hitler became chancellor on January 30, 1933, he could not immediately launch an aggressive foreign policy, but had to bide his time, consolidate his regime, and rearm the nation. Although, despite the provisions of the Versailles treaty, limited rearmament had been going on secretly during the Weimar period, the armed forces were still inadequate for the ambitions of the new chancellor. He did not conceal his goals from those whose support he needed. At a private dinner on February 3, 1933, he informed prominent members of the High Command that if Germany were to regain its position of power in Europe, the armed forces would have to be rebuilt by universal military conscription. Once the armed forces regained their strength, Germany would be able to acquire the much needed *Lebensraum* in eastern Europe.

Of course, the armed forces Hitler inherited could not be considered puny by any standards. In the dark days immediately following World War I, a brilliant staff officer Hans von Seeckt managed to keep the German army intact, thus easing Hitler's labors by laying the foundations for the mighty Wehrmacht. During the war, this aristocratic Prussian officer had helped achieve the breakthrough on the Russian front. After the war, in 1920, when he was appointed chief of the Army Command, he was given greater authority than any previous military commander in German history. Seeckt immediately set out to rebuild the army within the limitations of the Versailles treaty, making preparations for further expansion once Germany was free of the treaty.

Because of his negative attitude toward the Weimar Republic, Seeckt had created his army as a state within a state, an enemy of the Republic but a servant of "Germany." As such, there were subtle ways the army was able to get around the treaty provisions. Although the treaty had abolished military training schools, Seeckt managed to turn the army into one great school, not only training the enlisted men but also encouraging the officers to formulate new tactical doctrines, study foreign military thought, and produce studies on the uses of new weapons. To avoid the restrictions the treaty placed on armaments, Seeckt had established secret arms depots that could be moved whenever necessary to escape detection by the Allied Control Commission. He had joined with the Krupp munitions firm to develop plans for new kinds of artillery, armor plating, anti-aircraft guns, and tanks. Through secret arrangements with the Soviet government, he had managed a pilot training school, a tank school, an aircraft factory, a poison gas factory, and a shell factory all on Russian soil. The General Staff, strictly forbidden by the treaty, managed to continue functioning by camouflaging its activities in government ministries, civilian offices, and the Truppenamt (troop office) of the army.

If it had not been for the efforts of this military genius, Hitler's plans probably would have taken much longer than they did. As it was, Hitler's eagerness to build the army could not be restrained. On February 8, only nine days after Hitler had taken over as chancellor, his cabinet learned that he was negotiating with the Allied powers to nullify the armaments section of the Versailles treaty to obtain equality in armaments for Germany. But what Hitler was aiming at was full rearmament—superiority, not equality. Once Germany possessed sufficient weapons and trained troops to alter the balance of power in Europe, Hitler could ignore the Versailles treaty entirely.

The greatest obstacle Hitler faced in achieving this end was the Geneva Disarmament Conference, which had opened in February of the previous year after many years of debate, wrangling, and planning. In that year preceding Hitler's ascendancy, Germany's representatives had been, first, Chancellor Heinrich Bruening himself and, later, Chancellor Franz von Papen's emissary, General Werner von Blomberg. Nevertheless, Hitler made himself felt at the conference. Bruening, soon to fall from power but desperately trying to hold on to his office, gave in to the Nazi pressure to take a hard line at the conference by insisting that all nations join Germany in "disarmament." But Hitler did not have to pressure Blomberg, who would later be his Minister of Defense and who was already enjoying the future Fuehrer's confidence.

The "equality" in armaments sought by Germany at the conference was aimed not so much at achieving disarmament by the other countries as at acquiring recognition by these countries of Germany's equal position among nations. After all, it was a full member of the League of Nations: should it have restrictions placed on it that were not placed on other nations?

In September 1932, because the German claim had not been recognized in principle, the German delegation withdrew from the conference. The major powers had second thoughts and quickly moved to appease the Germans. On December 11, they promised Germany "equality of rights in a system which would provide security for all nations."

When the German delegation rejoined the conference in February 1933, it was in a full sense Hitler's delegation; once gratified in its demands, it was ready to push on for more.

The promise of equality of armaments between France and Germany—restricting the land armies to the same size—would not satisfy Hitler. Nor was he satisfied with the five-year period for disarmament prescribed by British Prime Minister Ramsay MacDonald's plan. Hitler wanted worldwide disarmament, effected in less time. He warned the conference that, if other nations did not disarm, Germany would insist on rebuilding its army to equal size. Part of his reason for this move was to provoke France—which would be relegated to an army of 200,000 with an overseas force of 200,000—to strenuous objection, thereby wrecking the conference altogether.

When the conference resumed in the fall of 1933 after a brief recess, the French presented a new plan that called for a four-year freeze on armaments while disarmament supervision was tested. If the supervision were successful, then all the powers would disarm in the following four years, making disarmament take up an eight-year period in total. Neither the inspection nor the eight years were palatable to Hitler. When Britain, the United States, and Italy supported the French plan, Hitler was backed into a corner. The supervision of the disarmament would uncover German violations of the Versailles treaty, and the eight-year period could not be adjusted to German industrial needs.

On October 14, Hitler announced German withdrawal from the Disarmament Conference and from the League of Nations as well, contending that equality of rights had been withheld from the German people. He announced that Germany would rebuild its army to thirty-six divisions by conscription. At the same time, he dissolved the Reichstag, ordering a new election as a vote of confidence for his actions. And he challenged the major powers by informing them baldly that German national interests were not subject to international conferences. England, France, and Italy continued to try to resolve the difficulties with Germany, but to no avail. There was no way the Treaty of Versailles could be invoked against Hitler.

THE FOUR-POWER PACT

An attempt to deal with other aspects of the treaty revision also failed. In March 1933, Mussolini presented a plan for a European directorate to be composed of Italy, Germany, France, and Great Britain. This directorate would be responsible for maintaining the peace and for making necessary revisions in peace treaties. Mussolini's proposition belied his hopes for Italy. It favored the four powers to the disadvantage of the countries of eastern Europe. He thought that the pact would give him a free hand in Austria and Yugoslavia, and thus help to establish Italy permanently as a great power. By freeing Germany of the fetters of the Treaty of Versailles and giving it a position of equal power, Mussolini hoped to reassure himself that Hitler had no aggressive intentions toward Italy.

When the pact was finally signed in July, it had been watered down by French objections to be far less than Mussolini had hoped. The pact never had a chance to be effected, because, before the countries involved had a chance to ratify it, Germany withdrew from the League of Nations and the Disarmament

Conference. The only purpose it served finally was to turn Poland against France, thereby giving Hitler a new victory. Hurt by French failure to respond to its demands for equal position among the nations of Europe and tired of being used against Germany, Poland turned to Hitler for a pact that would, in effect, nullify its earlier pact with France. Poland promised that agreements with a third party (France) would not hinder peaceful relations with Germany; and both nations pledged to use peaceful means to reach a settlement if disputes arose. The pact would run until 1944. Hitler had achieved his first significant diplomatic victory.

THE DOLLFUSS AFFAIR

Hitler's luck failed him in his next endeavor outside German territory. Austria, under the leadership of Chancellor Engelbert Dollfuss, was a primary target for Hitler. German *Anschluss* (union) was necessary for German *Lebensraum*. Though it is probably true that Hitler had no direct involvement in the events in Austria in July of 1934, he must be considered indirectly responsible. He had expressed in *Mein Kampf* the need for *Anschluss*, and his radio had been broadcasting calls to Austria to rejoin Germany, by any means necessary, even murder.

The person standing in the way of achieving these goals, and thus the person Hitler hoped to see murdered, was Chancellor Dollfuss, a Christian Socialist who refused to accept all of the Nazis' demands. Never a lover of democracy, Dollfuss in March 1933 suspended Parliament because of a deadlock with the Social Democrats; ultimately, in May 1934, he banned political parties and promulgated a new authoritarian constitution. But urged on from Germany, Austrian Nazis demanded complete surrender to their demands, which would have given them control of the government. At the same time, they sabotaged Dollfuss's efforts to negotiate an agreement with them by initiating a campaign of terror.

Upset with Dollfuss and influenced by German radio propaganda, a small group of conspirators dressed in Austrian army uniforms took control of the Vienna chancellery on July 25, 1934, assassinating Dollfuss and announcing his resignation over the government radio. The coup was poorly organized and did not last long before the government was able to resume control. Presumably, the conspirators expected Hitler to come to their assistance, but circumstances were such that this was impossible.

When Hitler first received news of the coup, he was elated, and he listened carefully to the developments occurring in Vienna. Although he had his Austrian Legion poised along the Austrian border, Hitler hesitated to enter the country unless the coup was overwhelmingly successful. When news reached him that Italian troops had been rushed to the Brenner Pass to halt any German invasion, he knew he could take no action. Actually, no troops had been dispatched; those at the Brenner Pass were there simply on maneuvers. However, their presence had the effect of an Italian move. Immediately, Hitler's radio changed its tune from congratulating the Austrian revolutionaries to consoling the Austrian government.

Fearful of being involved with the unsuccessful conspirators, Hitler publicly condemned their actions. When he was further embarrassed by the fact that some German Nazis were involved in the affair, he tried to save face by ordering them to cease meddling in extra-national concerns. Though the failure of the Austrian coup did not have an effect on Hitler's goals, it forced him to alter his tactics somewhat, making him wait until he had a mighty German army at his command.

GERMANY'S MILITARY RENAISSANCE

After his success with Poland, Hitler again stated his policy to a selected audience of army and S.A.[2] leaders, informing them on February 28, 1934 that Germany would be faced with "frightful destruction" unless it could find sufficient living space for its

[2] From the word "Sturmabteilung," the storm troopers.

people. The living space, he suggested, was to be found to the east; but, because the western European powers would be certain to oppose him, he proposed to strike at the west first and then turn east. This effort, however, would require a massive army. He had two choices for achieving this: he could build upon the well-structured Reichswehr or he could turn to the youthful S.A. brawlers. In return for their support in making him dictator on the death of Hindenburg, he chose to award this honor to the Reichswehr. The S.A. and its ambitious leaders would have to be dispensable. He proved their dispensability on June 30 by liquidating those S.A. leaders who had challenged his plans.

Expansion of the armed forces required bringing some activities out into the open. Such things as the launching of warships and the testing of fighter planes could not be hidden for long. But Hitler restrained himself from denouncing the armament restrictions on Germany until after the Saar plebiscite in January 1935. This was the date set by the Treaty of Versailles for self-determination of the Saarlanders. Once they had voted solidly in favor of returning to Germany, Hitler could begin to reveal his military activities.

On March 9, 1935, the German government announced the existence of the German air force. Then, when the French government doubled the term of service and lowered the age of enlistment to compensate for the lower birth rate in the years from 1914 to 1918, Hitler had an excuse for his next action. On March 16, he announced conscription and a thirty-six division army. Military rebirth was hailed by the German people with great joy. Once more, Hitler's popularity soared. Germany's wartime enemies, from whom Hitler had expected hostile reactions, were fearful of provoking another world war and consequently did nothing to stop him. Short of war, little could have been done. When Sir John Simon and Anthony Eden visited Germany later that month, they protested mildly about the air force and suggested joint efforts at coming to some sort of disarmament agreement. But, Hitler taunted his guests with the comment—

later proved to be a lie—that the German air force had already achieved parity with the R.A.F., and that he would in no way be interested in giving up that position.

Both Britain and France issued statements of protest and began to take steps toward rearmament, but they were reluctant efforts in comparison to those of Germany. As usual, the other European powers turned to conferences and joint statements to reassure themselves that peace would continue, blindly believing that talk would make action unnecessary. In April, Pierre Laval, the new French premier, met with MacDonald and Mussolini in Stresa, Italy, where they solemnly announced opposition to "any unilateral repudiation of treaties which may endanger the peace of Europe." To further console themselves, they reaffirmed their obligations as outlined by the treaty of Locarno. The Stresa Front, as this united action was labeled, was widely heralded as a barrier to Hitler.

But this action would prove insufficient to deter the massive moves of the German Fuehrer. Hitler was building a weaponry that would enable Germany to win by *Blitzkrieg*—surprise attack, swift invasion, exploitation of the confusion, and quick victory. As long as he had such superiority in weapons, Hitler did not need a superiority in numbers of troops. He preferred this kind of warfare because it achieved his goal swiftly—i.e., restoring Germany to world power—with only a portion of the economy geared to war. Total rearmament—troops as well as weapons—would require a complete overhaul of the economy, thereby frightening the country and shaking its faith in the Fuehrer. He hoped to avoid world war, because world war would mean austerity for the German people, and he knew that the German people wanted prosperity.

Just as a weapons superiority was suited to the German economy, the new German army and the German geographical location were suited to *Blitzkrieg* warfare. Surrounded by weak nations too often interested only in quarreling with each other, Germany could move in lightning attacks and acquire territories one-by-one without giving the other major powers time to object. And, as long as Germany did not have a massive army, the major powers would not have reason to fear it.

Opposition to this military policy of Hitler's did develop later. Some army officers were disturbed that, if the conflict burgeoned into a world war of the proportions of that of 1914–1918, the German army would not be prepared. (Essentially, this is why Hitler would finally be defeated.) Hitler, however, opposed the long-range economic planning that this required. As long as the men surrounding him depended on orders issued without warning, Hitler knew he was in control. Long-range economic planning and rearmament for world war could create powerful vested interests that would oppose his dictatorship. With time to think, there would be the possibility that someone else could gain control of the economy, and whoever controlled the economy would be a threat to his power. He would not be willing to make preparations for a world war until forced into them by circumstances.

It was in the summer of 1936 that Hitler inaugurated his short-range four-year economic plan that would lessen German dependency on foreign sources for raw materials and would make the army and the economy ready for his *Blitzkrieg* program. His plans would find fruition: by 1939, he would have adequate forces for a short war against a smaller nation, but these forces would be inadequate for the major war involving the United States and the Soviet Union that he would be confronted with two years later.

THE FRANCO-RUSSIAN PACT

One of the peculiarities of the period was the French dependency on treaties, alliances, and pacts. Just as it was characteristic of the Germans to turn to the military, it was characteristic of the French that they sought solution to their security problems—and perhaps created a few, as well—through alliances.

Hitler's renunciation of the disarmament clauses of the Treaty of Versailles brought on talks between France and the Soviet Union that eventually led to the Franco-Russian Alliance. From October 1933, when Joseph Paul-Boncour as French Foreign Minister first proposed a mutual assistance pact to Maxim Litvinov, the Soviet Commissar for Foreign Affairs, until May 1935, when the pact was finally signed, the negotiations took a strange and circuitous path.

After Hitler ordered his delegates to leave the Geneva Disarmament Conference, Paul-Boncour approached Litvinov with the suggestion that, since Russia had just joined the League of Nations and France had developed an intricate alliance system in Europe, it would be to the advantage of both nations to come to some sort of agreement. Before serious negotiations began, however, Paul-Boncour was turned out of office, along with the rest of the government, because of a government scandal.

The Foreign Minister who took office in February 1934 was a conservative lawyer named Louis Barthou. In continuing the negotiations with Russia, Barthou chose to tie the Franco-Russian alliance to an eastern Locarno Pact—that is, a treaty of regional assistance that would involve Russia, Germany, Poland, Czechoslovakia, Finland, Estonia, Latvia, and Lithuania. It was shortly before this that Poland and Germany had signed their non-aggression pact, taking both France and Russia by surprise. But it was Russia that was most alarmed at the event; for Russia had been imagining that it and Germany shared a hostility for the Treaty of Versailles as well as a similar hatred for the Poles. All efforts at international agreement suddenly appeared to be in upheaval. Stalin's attempts to foster better relations with Germany had been rebuffed by Hitler; Germany rejected an eastern European alliance; Poland considered it a blow to its imagined big-power status; France gave up trying to get Germany to disarmament talks; and Italy and Britain were critical of the proposed alliance system. Finally, in September 1934, efforts at achieving an eastern Locarno Pact petered out, leaving Barthou and Litvinov with only the proposed Franco-Russian Alliance.

But, before Barthou could conclude the pact, he was killed in Marseilles when Croatian terrorists assassinated King Alexander of Yugoslavia. Later, a great deal of reverence was paid to Barthou as the only man who might have been able to stiffen French resistance to Hitler, but such reverence is exaggerated: the revolving cabinet system soon would have pushed him out of office, replacing him with someone less resolute. Actually, Barthou's projects in Europe were insufficient for the needs of France; whatever strengths they possessed would have been dissipated by problems of geography and mutual suspicion among nations.

Finally, it was left to the most unlikely prospect, Pierre Laval, to bring the Franco-Russian Alliance into existence. Laval, a wealthy lawyer who had been a defeatist in World War I, had slight interest in either the eastern alliance system or in any agreement with the Soviet Union. Rather, he dreamed of preserving peace by uniting Britain, Italy, and France in an effort to entice Hitler into a four-power directorate of Europe. When, on March 16, 1935, Hitler wrecked Laval's plans by announcing conscription for building the German army, the French cabinet panicked and forced Laval into concluding the Pact of Mutual Assistance with Russia.

The pact, signed on May 2, 1935, appeared to face Germany with a war on two fronts if either France or Russia were attacked, but the Franco-Russian security was only on paper. Certainly, each promised the other mutual aid in case of unprovoked attack, but not until both nations had taken the matter to the Council of the League of Nations. Any military action had to wait until they were faced with failure by the Council to reach a unanimous decision. To further complicate matters, action under the terms of the pact could not violate other treaty obligations, such as the Locarno Pact. This meant that, whatever action it was to undertake, France first must have obtained the approval of the Locarno powers—most important, Great Britain. The final fault of the pact was one that Russia hoped to exploit: the band of states that separated Germany from Russia was a barrier to any Russian attack on Germany. The troops of the Soviet Union would have to pass through lands that the czars had once governed. The pact did not indicate how such passage was to be accomplished. France could not be bothered with such a minor problem.

Neither could it be bothered with working out the military details of the pact. Both countries had agreed to a military convention that would determine the tasks of each army, but France seemed to feel that the alliance alone would suffice to divide the German army between east and west, thereby permitting the French troops in the Maginot Line to fend off attacks from a weakened invader. The military details, it felt, were minor matters. But the French reluctance to cooperate with the Russians was not entirely negligence. They had also been put off by Stalin's military purges of 1937 and by the rumors—later proved to have been fabricated by the Gestapo—of Russian intrigues with Nazi generals.

But, if France was unwilling to complete the alliance, it was to the detriment of France. Russia was achieving what it wanted from the pact. In 1934, Stalin had begun to wipe out all opposition to his rule. He accepted the pact because it might give the country limited protection while the internal power struggle raged. His ultimate aim in concluding the pact was to make Hitler more amenable toward making a deal. But, within a year, it became evident that Stalin needed nothing at all from the French alliance. Having tightened his hold on the government of the Soviet Union, Stalin had his emissaries seek to allay German fears that the pact was aimed at encircling Germany.

Actually, the pact proved to be of more use to Hitler than it was to the signatories. Not only did it provide him with the ammunition he needed for his speeches denouncing Russia and communism, but it also aided him in remilitarizing the Rhineland. The governments caught between Germany and Russia had had enough of Russian rule under the czars. Catching the implications of the pact, they turned toward Hitler as the only alternative.

THE ANGLO-GERMAN NAVAL AGREEMENT

The Baltic nations were not the only ones bothered by the Franco-Russian alliance. The British felt that this simply confirmed their suspicions of France, which seemed bent on encircling Germany. Britain still insisted that the best way to deal with Germany was to negotiate, believing that reasonable men could always be counted on to come to reasonable agreements. Because the British navy was feeling the strain of Britain's vast empire, its prime target was a limitation of the navy of one of its competitors—Germany.

The government of Ramsay MacDonald had been pressing for an agreement with Germany for some time. It had received encouragement from Hitler in November 1934, but when Simon and Eden visited Berlin for discussion with the Fuehrer in March 1935, he was not encouraging at all. MacDonald had hoped— and Hitler had fed his hopes—to limit Germany to 35 percent of the total fleet of the British Commonwealth, but Hitler now would not bargain over that figure. They were dismayed still further in April, when the announcement was made that Germany was building twelve destroyers, two cruisers, and twelve submarines.

Finally, on June 4, when representatives of the two governments met in London to negotiate an agreement, Joachim von Ribbentrop, under strict orders from Hitler, refused to make any concessions. The British wanted to make the agreement dependent on the approval of other major powers—primarily France— but Ribbentrop insisted on a bilateral agreement, threatening to break off the negotiations if it were not. Quickly, the British complied, leaving France in the cold.

On June 18, the 150th anniversary of the battle of Waterloo, the Anglo-German Naval Agreement was signed. Germany promised that the total tonnage of the German fleet would never exceed 35 percent of the aggregate tonnage of the combined fleets of the British Commonwealth, and was given the right to build up to 100 percent of the submarine strength of the British Commonwealth. The British had forsaken their insistence on limitation according to category of warship: Germany would not be hampered by restrictions on displacement and gun caliber, insisting on a straight limitation by ratio. Defenders of the agreement rationalized that, since Germany would rearm any-way, the British had to be more accommodating unless they were willing to halt rearmament by force. Any limitation that could be obtained on the German navy would relieve some of the strain on the British fleet spread thin around the Commonwealth. If Hit-ler willingly signed an agreement, Britain had little choice but to depend on him to observe it.

They did not realize fully how Hitler had won a brilliant victory. He had managed, by diplomacy, to shatter the Stresa Front and create distrust of Britain among its neighbors. He had succeeded in ending the naval provisions of the Versailles treaty through negotiations and a signed agreement, thereby proving that he could be reasonable. He had succeeded, where the government of Kaiser Wilhelm II had failed, to negotiate a major naval agreement with Germany's major naval opponent. But even further, to Hitler, the agreement revealed British will-ingness to protect its national interests at the expense of inter-national causes. Most important, the action had created French distrust of England, making cooperation between the two coun-tries difficult for some time.

The German victory did not go entirely unnoticed in En-gland; but the government was excused from the criticism because the cabinet of Stanley Baldwin was in the process of re-placing that of the aged MacDonald and thus could not have had the experience of dealing with such matters. It was the confusion of this transition, some argued, that had allowed them to approve the agreement. But the basis of the arrangement with Germany had been discussed by the two governments before the change. The new cabinet was quite positive in hoping to avoid a repetition of the naval race that had preceded World War I. The agreement would appeal to all who condemned the Treaty of Versailles and longed for armaments limitations. And, since the opposition was much concerned over this subject, an agreement with Germany would aid the government in the coming general election.

Actually, the agreement did not limit German naval construction as its defenders contended, but then, little would have prevented it were Hitler so inclined. What did limit the German navy were inadequacies in the industrial system, the lack of raw materials, and the demands of the German army and air force. The greater naval menace really lay in the Pacific with the Japanese fleet, whose building program Britain could not halt.

With the Anglo-German Naval Agreement, Hitler had finally succeeded in destroying all of the disarmament provisions of the Treaty of Versailles. And he had won his victories without firing a shot. But the succeeding years would prove that Hitler would use his easily gained "military equality" to gain further victories. Europe's years of peace were soon to end.

3 / Years of Crisis, 1935-1938

MUSSOLINI AND ETHIOPIA

Since 1921, when Poland and Russia made peace, there had been no war involving major European powers. But the peace came to an end in October 1935, when Italian armies sent by Benito Mussolini invaded Ethiopia. Mussolini originally had been an elementary schoolteacher, but his early career also included lecturing on atheism, dodging the draft, and often getting himself thrown into jails for advocating class warfare. His career took a step forward when he became director of *Avanti*, the official Socialist newspaper, but he accepted French bribes in 1914 to change the paper's policy from absolute neutrality to intervention. When Italy went to war, Mussolini was no longer able to avoid the draft. His army record lacked distinction, and he was finally invalided out of the army because of a slight wound from a mortar.

Forsaking socialism in 1919, he founded the *Fasci di Combattimento* (Fighting Group), the Fascist party, which would later terrorize northern Italy. In the fall of 1922, Mussolini, with the help of his party, threatened to overthrow the government. To avoid a civil war, King Victor Emmanuel III surrendered the country to Mussolini. The new dictator was a figure who appealed to businessmen fearful of communism, to frustrated

46

veterans, and to angry nationalists. However, he had no program for government, finding it advantageous to choose his ideology as needs arose.

Mussolini actually lacked physical courage, though he tried to appear to be a superman. He was a notorious lecher and he was also vindictive and cruel, driven by selfish ambition. But often when he met foreigners, he would turn on the charm and they would come away believing that he was a dynamic leader, resolute in action and firm in making decisions. Actually he was a fraud, nothing more than a superstitious peasant fearful of the evil eye, indecisive, and shaken by fears and prejudices. No one spoke more nonsense about politics or made more false predictions about foreign affairs.

A vain and arrogant man, he was ignorant not only about his government but about his own armed forces as well. As late as 1939, he still did not know accurately the actual size of the Italian air force. He accepted quite seriously the suggestion of Count Galeazzo Ciano, his Foreign Minister and son-in-law, that the prefects count the planes on the airfields within their prefectures to determine his air strength. Figures so impressed him that when Goering informed him that Germany had 80 million tins of canned food to withstand the British blockade, he was reassured of Germany's strength, not stopping to think that, in 1939, it meant only one tin of food for each German citizen.

He was also naive in his appraisal of Hitler, whom he disliked as a man but admired as a dictator. Hitler's strength of purpose and willpower so fascinated Mussolini that he could not bring himself to question Hitler or to bargain with him. To the bitter end, he believed in Hitler's word. But he was also jealous of Hitler, and it was his jealousy that drove him into foreign adventures that Italy could not afford.

Mussolini's foreign policy had no logic, only drift and vacillation. He despised Britain and France because their pacifism seemed weak to him, but he was jealous of their wealth and status. Childishly, Mussolini dreamed of reestablishing a Roman

Empire around the Mediterranean—a status symbol his dreams told him he could acquire cheaply and quickly. Ethiopia would be the first addition. By taking the small African country, he would also be avenging the disgrace of Adowa, where in 1896, Ethiopian troops had defeated the Italian army. By succeeding in a short war with an abundance of military glory, he would be able to divert the attention of the Italian public from their economic miseries and impress both Hitler and Europe. He had no qualms about attacking another member of the League of Nations—and, at that, a country he had originally sponsored for membership.

He began his preparations for war in 1932, but he had no excuse to start it until November 1934, when a British commission delimiting the Ethiopian border along the frontiers of British and Italian Somaliland reached the outpost at Walwal, inside Ethiopian borders. Since 1930, it had been garrisoned by Italian forces because of the importance of the nearby wells— the sources of life in the region. An Ethiopian military force, which had joined the commission earlier, now set up camp near the Italian outpost. Because of the tense situation, the commission withdrew on November 25, leaving the two military forces separated by a line of brushwood about six feet wide. On the afternoon of December 5, shots were fired and a short battle took place. Although the Ethiopians suffered the heavier casualties and fled from Walwal, Mussolini demanded an apology, a heavy indemnity, and the recognition of Italian control of the disputed region. Emperor Haile Selassie was pressured by Britain and France to accede to Mussolini's demands, but he refused, realizing that accession would only encourage Mussolini to make further demands. Instead, the Emperor requested arbitration of the affair, and when Mussolini refused the request, he brought his case before the League of Nations.

The Emperor's action embarrassed the British and French, but more important, it infuriated the Italians, who did not want the League interfering with their bullying. Although the incident was a little ahead of his schedule, it spurred Mussolini to speed up his preparations for war to settle relations between Ethiopia and Italy. On December 20, he ordered his associates to prepare Italy for a war of conquest that would commence no later' than October 1935.

If there was to be any effective opposition to Mussolini's aggression, it would have to come from Britain or France, which were the only countries to have bases in Africa that could be used to mount a campaign against Italy. But the three nations had signed an agreement in 1906 that committed them all to maintain the *status quo* in Ethiopia and to avoid unilateral action.

Mussolini settled the Ethiopian question with France on January 7, 1935, when Laval, in an exchange of letters renounced French economic interests in Ethiopia. But more important, he gave Mussolini a verbal promise of a free hand in Ethiopia, assuming that, once bought off, the Italian dictator would side with France against Germany. Laval fancied that a union of France and Italy could command respect from Hitler and entice him into the old four-power directorate with the British. On January 29, when he informed Britain of his economic arrangement with France, Mussolini hinted that he had more than a passing interest in Ethiopia. His purpose was to invite the British to discuss the Ethiopian question to prepare them for the coming war. These overtures were made to Foreign Secretary Sir John Simon, who soon realized that Mussolini was bent on war. Simon had no special liking for Ethiopia, and if British opposition to Mussolini's policies were to endanger the Fascist regime in Italy, Simon wanted no part of it. Because of British strategic needs in the Mediterranean, he preferred Italy as a friend rather than an enemy. Simon did not believe that protection of Ethiopia was worth endangering Anglo-Italian relations, and he was certainly not going to risk them by supporting the League of Nations. He could have brought Mussolini to bargain over Ethiopia if he had acted; but, because Simon did nothing, Mussolini interpreted his silence as approval.

An opportunity to set forth the British position on Ethiopia came when Mussolini met with MacDonald, Laval, and Simon at Stresa in April 1935 for the purpose of creating a common front against Germany. Experts on Ethiopia from both London and Paris were present, but there was no discussion whatsoever of Ethiopia. Mussolini had come expecting meaningful talks on this situation, but MacDonald and Simon avoided them deliberately. At last, Mussolini brought the subject up indirectly in a discussion concerning a sentence to appear in the final communiqué. It read, "The three powers, the object of whose policy is the collective maintenance of peace within the framework of the League of Nations, find themselves in complete agreement in opposing, by all practicable means, any unilateral repudiation of treaties which may endanger the peace. . . ." Mussolini asked if the words "of Europe" should not be inserted at this point. Twice he repeated the question; and each time, he was answered by silence, which he interpreted as assent. Mussolini therefore inserted the words in the communiqué, certain that he had British support for his Ethiopian war. Actually, Simon and MacDonald had no policy for Ethiopia, but they gave Mussolini their silent acquiescence in order to get him to join in the Stresa Front against Hitler.

The attitude of Simon and MacDonald was supported in Britain by diehard British imperialists, who sympathized with Mussolini, and by a group—led by Robert Vansittart, Permanent Under-Secretary in the Foreign Office—who preferred not to antagonize the Italian dictator in hopes of luring him away from Hitler. However, the latter group had exaggerated Mussolini's proprietary concern for Austria. They believed that a Nazi threat to Austria would be met by fierce resistance from Mussolini, but this proved to be an inaccurate appraisal. Although Mussolini had coveted Austria as an Italian satellite, Ethiopia was now more important to him. He was willing to surrender Austria to Hitler in return for German neutrality in the Ethiopian affair. It is a testament to the Duce's diplomatic ability that he succeeded in fooling the political "realists" into thinking that he might possibly have chosen to ally himself with Britain and France rather than with Nazi Germany.

In June 1935, in Britain, a pioneer effort in sampling public opinion called the "Peace Ballot" was published. Its results were surprising to the "realists" as well as to the other politicians. While it had originated as a means of making Britain more conscious of the League of Nations, its effect was to imply widespread support for the concept of collective security as well as for the League of Nations. Over 11½ million people participated in the poll—almost as many as had voted in the general election of 1931. Almost all of those polled were in favor of Britain remaining within the League of Nations and of using economic, non-military sanctions against aggressors. Over 6½ million of those polled favored military sanctions (the use of force) if necessary, and only 2½ million of them were opposed to military sanctions. Another 2½ million abstained from expressing any opinion on the question. The Peace Ballot had the effect of persuading the Baldwin government, which was then facing a general election, to display more enthusiasm for the League of Nations than they had before.

Anthony Eden, minister without portfolio for the League of Nations, traveled to Rome in June 1935 to offer Mussolini a deal —if the dictator would accept only a certain area of Ethiopian territory, Britain would give British territory in Africa to Haile Selassie as compensation. But Eden had come too late with too little. Mussolini scorned the offer, informing Eden that Laval had already given him *carte blanche* in Ethiopia. Either he would have all of what he wanted in Ethiopia peacefully or he would take it by force. It is likely that Mussolini had already seen the Maffey report, which had been commissioned in January by the Foreign Office to study British interests in Ethiopia.

Although it was not released to the public, Mussolini's agents photographed it in the British embassy in Rome. The report stated: "No vital British interests exist in Ethiopia or adjoining countries sufficient to oblige His Majesty's Government to resist a conquest of Ethiopia by Italy. . . . It is a matter of indifference whether Ethiopia remains independent or is absorbed by Italy."

Having had their bargain rejected, and faced with a general election at home and with Italy preparing for war, the British government decided to take a stand behind the League and in favor of collective security—if all other countries would follow suit. This ingenious solution was the idea of Sir Samuel Hoare, now the Foreign Secretary, who in speaking to the League Assembly on September 11 declared, "The League stands, and my country stands with it, for the collective maintenance of the Covenant, . . . and particularly for steady and collective resistance to all acts of unprovoked aggression. . . . If the burden is to be borne, it must be borne collectively. If risks for peace are to be run, they must be run by all. The security of the many cannot be ensured solely by the efforts of a few, however powerful they may be." This statement made Hoare the hero of all believers in the League's "collective security." His statement, a bluff that had the full approval of Baldwin, was aimed at British voters in the impending general election.

However, Hoare weakened the effect of his statement by secretly agreeing with Laval that military sanctions—the only action that could deter Mussolini—were too dangerous for Europe. At most, they would be willing to agree to the cautious application of economic sanctions. Hoare went even further in vitiating the impact of his speech by assuring Mussolini, in a personal message on September 23, that Britain had no intention of harming him or interfering with his country's interests and would refrain from applying military sanctions or closing the Suez Canal. Mussolini was now free to begin his war.

On October 3, without a declaration of war, Italy invaded

Ethiopia. The League of Nations Assembly met and voted in favor of economic sanctions against Italy, but they left the implementation of the sanctions to the judgment of the League members. Most of the League members did place a ban on all exports to Italy and on most Italian imports but no nation wished to commit itself to more pressure than any other nation. No one dared to suggest blocking the Suez Canal, because the canal fell within British jurisdiction, and Britain did not want to commit itself to such an action. Britain's hesitancy was based on the fear that Mussolini might attempt some foolish act, such as bombing Malta or Alexandria. Since the Chiefs of Staff had advised the cabinet that the fleet in the Mediterranean had insufficient strength to defend itself and that the nation was unprepared for war, Britain would not take provocative action.

Mussolini heightened the fears of the sanctioning nations. He threatened war if Italy were faced with oil sanctions; and his threats were taken very seriously in Paris, where Laval labored on Mussolini's behalf, and in London, where the government realized that no other League member would assist the British navy in enforcing an oil embargo. Although the Baldwin government did win the general election on a platform of support for the League and for collective security, they had no intention of supporting it to the extent of going to war. Rather, they joined with Laval in seeking a compromise arrangement. British and French diplomats reached a solution early in December. It was with the full approval of the British cabinet that Hoare traveled to Paris to complete the agreement that would leave Haile Selassie with only a fragment of his empire.

Before his departure, Hoare had been repeatedly lectured by Baldwin, "Sam, keep us out of war, we are not ready for it." [1] On December 8, after two days of negotiation, Laval and Hoare initialed the document that is known to history as the Hoare–Laval Pact. It stipulated that Haile Selassie must cede a large portion of Ethiopia to Mussolini; the remainder of the country would become an Italian "sphere of influence." During the negotiations, Laval was in direct telephone communication with Mussolini, but the Ethiopian Emperor was kept in ignorance of this bargain. Baldwin's cabinet approved the draft and promptly forwarded it to Geneva for League consideration.

When details of the Pact leaked from the Quai d'Orsay to the French newspapers, a storm began to gather in the British Parliament over betrayal of the League. The uproar so frightened Baldwin that—despite the fact that his government had approved the Pact—he forced Hoare to accept full blame for the Pact and resign from office.

Neither the League nor Haile Selassie would accept the Pact, but Laval had achieved his goal—the League's oil sanctions were never enforced. Mussolini's armies completed their conquest of Ethiopia without opposition.

Both London and Paris had imagined that the Hoare–Laval Pact could entice Mussolini—by bribing him with Ethiopia—into opposing Hitler. But Mussolini had no inclination to oppose Hitler for Britain and France, whom he loathed. In making their assessment of the situation in the Mediterranean, London had exaggerated Italian prowess. The professionals in the Foreign Office, though not appeasement-minded, did not consider Ethiopia worth a major war. However, Robert Vansittart, Permanent Under-Secretary in the Foreign Office, who urged a tough line against Hitler, pushed for the Pact as a means of securing Italian support against Germany.

Baldwin used the issue of collective security as long as he needed it to win votes; but, once the election was safely past, he demanded peace and appeasement. He knew that sanctions, if truly enforced, would result in war, which neither he nor the nation desired, and he knew he could expect no help from the League of Nations. Also, there was the risk of a quarrel with the United States if British warships stopped American tankers carrying oil to Italy. Although the public had voted for collective security, Baldwin knew very well that the public would not support a war over Ethiopia. It was the politicians who had created the uproar over the Hoare–Laval Pact, particularly politicians who had nothing to lose by being indignant over the rejection of Ethiopia and the League. However, these idealists were unwilling to face the truth—that the only alternative to going to war with Mussolini was to make the best possible deal with him.

The movement in Britain in favor of collective security had its greatest support among the liberals, but they were vague about the meaning of "collective security." They never interpreted it to be a military alliance with plans for landing troops in Italy and marching on Rome. Nor did they see it as British Tommies moving into Ethiopia to protect the country from Italian troops. Instead, they dreamed that it was possible to halt armies by voting resolutions.

At the Munich Conference in 1938, Mussolini admitted to Hitler that a strict enforcement of oil sanctions by all the League members would have compelled him to withdraw from Ethiopia within a week. However, if Mussolini really believed his bluff would be met, he was underrating human greed. Despite the oil sanctions, Mussolini would have been able to purchase sufficient oil from the United States and other non-League nations to offset the sanctions. And further, if the British Admiralty attempted to enforce a naval blockade, they would be faced with the possibility of having to sink American tankers carrying oil to Italy.

Mussolini's armies continued the conquest of Ethiopia without interference because none of the members of the League would fight to enforce the Covenant. No nation would go to war over Ethiopia because no nation could feel that its vital national interests were at stake. Therefore, no nation mobilized in behalf of Ethiopia, nor did any nation move troops or ships to aid Emperor Haile Selassie's soldiers—except for the few British ships that were sent to the Mediterranean to watch out for British interests.

The failure of the League members to compel Mussolini to halt his invasion, which was clearly contrary to the Covenant, doomed the League of Nations. Yet the members were not wholly at fault because the challenge presented by the Italo-Ethiopian war had been undreamed of by the authors of the Covenant. They had never expected the League, because of a poorly drawn frontier, to make war in order to defend an African people against a European nation. Of course the League had never been designed as a means of uniting its members in an alliance to halt premeditated aggression.

War in 1935 would not necessarily have prevented the catastrophe that was to come. In fact, it could have precipitated it sooner. For later events were to prove that small preventive wars, instead of halting aggression, only served to bring on more. For example, the German invasion of Poland, by occupying the attention of Britain and France, gave Soviet Russia the opportunity to attack Finland. Had British soldiers battled Italian armies in Africa in 1935, Hitler would have been free to move troops into Central Europe, just as he would do later. As it turned out, the Italo-Ethiopian war, because of the strain on Anglo-French relations, offered Hitler an opportunity to move troops into the demilitarized Rhineland, thereby wrecking the Locarno Pact and ending another restriction in the Treaty of Versailles.

HITLER IN THE RHINELAND

Critics of appeasement have argued that Hitler's aggression should have been halted on March 7, 1936, when he ordered German troops into the demilitarized Rhineland. At that time, they suggest, while Britain and France still had the advantage, he could have been defeated. A display of force, perhaps only a division dispatched into the Rhineland, would have caused Hitler's generals to panic and would have obliged Hitler to recall his troops. Surely a revolution would have followed, he would have been overthrown and there would never have been a

World War II. However, aggression is not halted so easily; and even limited force is subject to escalation.

These critics forget that in 1936, because of guilt over the Versailles treaty and because of the loathing of the war, it would have been an arduous—if not an impossible—task to arouse the British and French peoples to fight a war over German soldiers occupying German territory.

Under the terms of the Versailles treaty, the Rhineland was to be forever demilitarized—no troops and no fortifications. The German government acknowledged this prohibition at Locarno. In his speech of May 21, 1935, Hitler paid his obeisance to the Locarno Pact, implying that he would accept a demilitarized Rhineland. But he was already contemplating occupation, a fact that London and Paris would know in time to plan united action.

After an interview with Hitler on November 21, 1935, André Francois-Poncet, the French ambassador, advised the Quai d'Orsay that Hitler had condemned the Franco-Soviet Pact and had indicated an intention to retaliate by occupying the Rhineland. On December 13, Hitler went even further by informing the British ambassador that he could easily have occupied the Rhineland in March 1935, but had then been content with maintaining the Locarno Pact. More concrete information on Hitler's intentions followed. Early in January 1936, the Swiss General Staff warned Paris of an impending move by German troops into the demilitarized zone. Two German army corps were also discovered suspiciously close to the demilitarized zone. The information was passed on to the French military attaché in Berlin, who was not surprised: he had suspected that the Germans would occupy the zone; only the date was in doubt.

The signs of military activity along the borders of the demilitarized zone so alarmed the French consul in Cologne that he returned to Paris to report. The rumors were that German troops would be in Cologne within three months, but he also had more concrete information. Military offices, headed by retired officers, were being established in the zone. Housing had been set aside for staff headquarters. In the demilitarized zone, fortifications were being strengthened, gun emplacements erected, barracks prepared for troops, and areas indicated as off limits to civilians. Motorized units of the German army had been moved up to the edge of the demilitarized zone. Every sign pointed to invasion, but no one knew when it might occur. Despite all these threats, the French General Staff did not wish to take any action. Its inertia could be overcome only by strong civilian leadership.

Unfortunately, on January 22, a caretaker government took office until the general election in the spring. It was headed by Albert Sarraut, once Governor-General of Indo-China, a man-about-town and lover of Paris night life, definitely not the man for a critical confrontation with Germany. His Foreign Minister, Pierre Flandin, politely asked for recommendations from the War Ministry in case Germany attempted to alter the status of the demilitarized zone. He hoped that, once acquainted with the military plans, he could talk with London and then send a joint Anglo-French warning to Berlin, thereby forcing negotiation of a solution to the Rhineland question.

But the generals were loath to shoulder the responsibility that ought to have belonged to the civilian ministers. At last, Minister of War, General Louis Marin, advised Flandin and the cabinet that it would be contrary to French interests to occupy the demilitarized zone, because it would make France appear the aggressor, alone and bereft of allies. According to Marin, any French occupation of the Rhineland should be planned only in full agreement with the British. He proposed to alert the troops on the frontiers, to strengthen the fortresses there, and to call up reservists and warn the air force; but he ruled out any French occupation of the demilitarized zone. As an "aggressor," in that case, under the Locarno Pact, France would lose all her allies, including Britain.

On February 19, after the Chiefs of Staff had taken up the matter, General Maurice Gamelin presented their conclusions.

If Germany were to occupy the right bank of the Rhine, France must not reoccupy the remainder or even a portion of the area, but must simply take precautionary measures. He advocated keeping the zone demilitarized until France could regain the population it had lost in the years between 1914 and 1918. Although he did not believe that France could prevent Germany forever from doing what it wished within its frontiers, he believed that they should hold the line until 1940. By February 25, the French War Ministry was sure of what it had been suspecting—that, once the Franco-Soviet Pact had been ratified, Hitler would consider Germany to be free of its obligations under the Locarno Pact; complete occupation of the Rhineland would follow immediately.

Two days later, the Sarraut government came to its decision: French troops would not confront German troops in the Rhineland. French soldiers would not enter the demilitarized zone unless the other Locarno powers dispatched troops. If German forces violated the zone, France would contact the other Locarno powers in order to take concerted action; but, until then, the government could take only precautionary measures. This decision to avoid a confrontation had a practical basis. To bring off an effective confrontation, France required an aggressive, professional military force, ready to sweep into the Rhineland and seize important strongholds while driving out the invaders. But France lacked this kind of army, although a Major Charles de Gaulle had proposed such an outfit and the military establishment had scorned his ideas to favor Marshal Petain's dogma that a good defense was preferable to a good offense.

Under the circumstances of 1936, the French General Staff made the only decision possible—to remain on the defensive, man the Maginot Line, and await the German attack that was expected to follow the occupation of the Rhineland. In all truth, the generals had no alternative. Their plans and the training and the troops necessitated such a strategy. The French General Staff, with the approval of the government and the nation, had aleady written off the Rhineland when they developed the Maginot Line. This massive defensive complex required that French troops stay within France. Because they had placed their emphasis on the Maginot Line, the General Staff did not draft plans for an invasion of the Rhineland.

In London, French reluctance was welcomed favorably. The British cabinet had been more fearful of the French reaction to a German occupation of the Rhineland than of the occupation itself. The British resented the Franco-Soviet Pact because it gave the Germans an excuse to be unpleasant. They also saw in the pact an indication of a French turn towards Russia and away from Britain. This is not to say that the British wanted an ally, but that they wanted the right of veto over French action.

Anthony Eden, the Foreign Secretary, who had succeeded Hoare, told the French that, because the Rhineland did not endanger British security, the responsibility for the zone lay with the French and Belgians. Rather than fight, Eden preferred to bargain with Hitler over the Rhineland as long as something remained to bargain away. Eden's ideas were in conformity with those of Prime Minister Stanley Baldwin, who refused any risk, believing that Hitler would not withdraw his troops if they were forced to fight for the Rhineland.

While London and Paris waited, Hitler acted. By February 12, Hitler had resolved to reoccupy the Rhineland. If successful, his popularity would soar and German security would be strengthened by having German troops on the French frontier. On the basis of military gain alone, the occupation was worth the risk to Germany. Hitler's decision was also influenced by the attitudes of the Locarno powers. Mussolini promised to do nothing if Hitler wished to react to the ratification of the Franco-Soviet Pact. From London came reports that the Foreign Office was seeking an agreement with Germany, despite the newspaper stories about the German threat to the Rhineland. France, caught in the depths of economic depression, was facing a general election campaign that would restrict public interest in foreign affairs.

For one reason or another, all the major powers who had pledged themselves under the Locarno Pact to insure a demilitarized Rhineland were ready to violate their pledges.

Hitler made it easier for them to violate the treaty by capitalizing on its defects. At the time the treaty was drafted, remilitarization of the Rhineland was considered a prelude to German attack on Belgium and France. Each treaty member was obligated to come to the aid of another if a frontier had been crossed, if hostilities had commenced, or if forces were assembling for an invasion. Hitler, in ordering his troops to ocupy the Rhineland, emphasized that they must appear to be peacetime soldiers taking up a permanent garrison in their own country, which indeed they were. To assist the British, Italians, and Belgians in evading their obligations, the appearance of all troop movements must be peaceful with no indication of an impending invasion.

But should this peaceful occupation encounter French forces, what then? The myth still persists, nurtured by the tales told at the Nuremberg trials, that German troops had orders to withdraw if they encountered opposition. It is implied that if French and Belgian forces had merely marched into the demilitarized zone, German soldiers would have immediately retreated without fighting, and Hitler would have been overthrown.

However, this was not the case. The standing orders, in force since Germany left the Disarmament Conference and the League of Nations in 1933, still prevailed: if foreign troops were encountered on German soil, they were to be considered as hostile and were to be repelled. Any withdrawal would be only a strategic retirement to a more defensible line. Hitler had no intention of recalling his troops across the Rhine if French or Belgian troops appeared. Unless he lost his nerve completely, any French resistance could only result in German troops fighting a war to drive out the invaders.

The opportunity Hitler had been waiting for came on February 27, when the French Chamber of Deputies approved the

Franco-Soviet Pact. Under orders from Hitler, Marshal Werner von Blomberg, Minister of War, issued the directive for the operation. Parts of three army corps would move up the Rhine, and three battalions would move further west, one to Aachen, one to Trier, and one to Saarbrücken. At the same time, anti-aircraft guns and Luftwaffe squadrons would be moved into the demilitarized zone, arriving at the same time as the three advance battalions. Marching orders would be delayed until the last minute in order to preserve security. If the enemy should violate the frontier with any offensive action, the standing orders would be put into effect. Meanwhile, orders to the fleet called for inconspicuous preparations, a submarine reconnaissance, equipping of U-boats for action in the English Channel and in the Atlantic, and strengthening of air defenses—in short, preparations for war.

Early on the morning of March 7, 1936, the three battalions crossed the Rhine heading for their assigned positions. About 9:45 AM that same morning, French military intelligence learned from two of its best sources that the occupation would most likely occur on March 12, March 15, or April 1. They would have been wiser to consult a French newspaper correspondent, for he was claiming that the German army units were already entering the demilitarized zone.

In Berlin at about 10:00 AM, Foreign Minister Constantine von Neurath told the ambassadors from the Locarno powers that Germany was denouncing their pact. In its place, Hitler offered a twenty-five-year non-aggression pact to France and Belgium and an air pact to Britain. He would accept a demilitarized zone only if it were redrawn on both sides of the frontier to give Germany and France equal treatment. For Germany's eastern neighbors, Hitler also had non-aggression pacts. To conclude his offer, Hitler announced his readiness to return to the League of Nations.

By noon, the German national police in the demilitarized zone, having undergone military training for months, were incorporated into the German army. About the same time in Berlin,

Hitler went before the Reichstag to declare Germany no longer bound by the Locarno Pact and to announce that the nation had taken full sovereignty over the Rhineland. At this news, the normally docile members of the Reichstag leaped to their feet, screaming approval and waving their hands in the Nazi salute. When the turmoil subsided, Hitler solemnly vowed not to yield to force and to strive for peace with the western powers. "We have no territorial demands to make in Europe," he declared. "Germany will never break the peace." [2] These were the words that Europe longed to hear.

Faced at last with the crisis that they had been expecting for months, the French politicians and the generals wasted five days in confused debate, and nothing was decided. The politicians refused to accept responsibility for ordering an invasion of the Rhineland. Because the French generals had convinced themselves that Germany had the advantage in numbers (which was not the case) and that any French invasion to end the occupation would mean war (which was the case), they reaffirmed their decision not to invade. However, they asked for general mobilization of the army in case a struggle should be forced upon them.

The French generals' request for a general mobilization has been denounced by their critics, but the generals had a legitimate case. For, in peacetime, the standing French army was only a skeleton force that had to be filled out with reservists to make the French army capable of fighting a war. This, too, was the reason that a force could not be hastily assembled from the standing army for an invasion of Germany. No units were ready to go into action intact until after the reservists had been mobilized.

Because the French cabinet was marking time until the general election, it did not want to order mobilization. And, too, the cabinet remembered the failure of their unilateral action in 1923, when French troops had occupied the Ruhr to collect repara-

2 William L. Shirer, *Berlin Diary* (New York, 1941), pp. 51–54.

tions. Then, London had disapproved; and, in 1936, London was offering no encouragement for a military action but was calling for appeasement. Unwilling to run the risk of incurring British censure again, the French cabinet ordered preparations to repel only a German attack on French territory, an attack which would never come.

Had there been an attack, some observers have argued that the French advantage in numbers of trained reserves would have meant Hitler's defeat. But they have exaggerated the possible effectiveness of these troops, forgetting that they were not all immediately available on March 7; and, too, numbers mean little without the will to use them boldly—a quality the French High Command lacked. Furthermore, the French army, untrained for a swift counterattack, would have needed time to mobilize and take up positions; and, while the French were mobilizing, the German forces would have had more time to increase and reinforce their hold on the Rhineland.

War surely would have come if French troops had entered the Rhineland; and the French High Command—which had written off the Rhineland long before March 7, 1936—would have been more defeatist than it was to be in 1940. And, if war had broken out then, French unity would have been severely strained, with voices on the right denouncing the war because it placed France on the side of Russia, and with pacifists on the left condemning a war whose purpose was to drive German troops out of German lands. More important to the French cabinet and generals, France would have been isolated.

On learning of the occupation, Eden indicated immediately that Britain would veto any French march into the Rhineland and would devote every effort to mediating between the belligerents. Actually relieved that the long-dreaded crisis had finally occurred, he was determined that it would be met without confrontation between France and Germany. He was following the lead of Baldwin, with whom he agreed, and who rejected every action that risked involving Britain in war. When Flandin personally proposed that Britain should support France in a police action, Baldwin replied: "You may be right, but if there is even one chance in a hundred that war would follow from your police operation, I have not the right to commit England. England is not in a state to go to war." [3] Baldwin's inaction met no protest from the House of Commons. Nor was he troubled by the average British voter, who had no appreciation of the significance of what was happening in the Rhineland. The British "man-on-the-street" could see only that Germany was reclaiming its own territory.

Because this action was so defensible, Hitler would not have recalled his troops. After committing the armed forces, a retreat would appear to the German people to be a betrayal and an admission of weakness. Had Britain and France fought in 1936, there is no indication that Hitler could have been overthrown by a revolt. The German people—even those Germans who dislike nazism—would have rallied behind Hitler in defense of the Fatherland, for his defense of German soil would have improved Hitler's image as a German patriot.

French Foreign Minister Flandin, confronted with the threat of an aroused Germany, with the handicap of reluctant French generals, and with no allies, decided to ask Hitler to evacuate the Rhineland while negotiations got underway. It would be understood that the result of the negotiations would be full German control of the Rhineland. Such a temperate policy delighted London, but the government in Paris vetoed Flandin's proposal without recommending a reasonable substitute. Finally, on March 19, the League Council assembled in London and condemned Germany's action as a violation of the Treaty of Versailles and the Locarno Pact; and with that action, the Council washed its hands of the matter. On the same day, the Locarno powers officially requested that Hitler stabilize the size of his occupation forces while presenting his case to them. If

[3] Winston Churchill, *The Gathering Storm* (Boston, 1948), p. 197.

he would cooperate with them, the Locarno powers—minus Italy —would negotiate his demands, officially revise the status of the Rhineland, and even draft a mutual assistance pact. When Hitler refused to negotiate, he was confronted with no further opposition.

With the remilitarization of the Rhineland, Hitler had demolished the last of the Versailles restrictions on Germany and had struck another blow at the French security system. By permitting German troops to enter the Rhineland unopposed, France had surrendered a vital military advantage. In addition, France had given *carte blanche* to Hitler to do whatever he wanted with French allies—if France would not fight when its own frontiers were threatened, it was unlikely that French troops would invade Germany when Poland and Czechoslovakia were under attack. Alarmed at French inaction in the face of the sudden growth of German power, the Belgian government chose permanent neutrality, rejecting military cooperation with France, a policy that had been followed since 1920. In April of 1937, Belgium was freed of all obligations under the Locarno Pact.

For France, the Rhineland occupation was the inevitable result of the weakness that had plagued the nation since 1919— the lack of an imaginative leadership. But the fault did not all lie with the French, for the British encouraged French inaction. Although postwar critics of Anglo-French policies have alleged that the Rhineland occupation was the last chance to deal with Hitler without bringing on a general war, this was not actually the case. Police action alone would not have succeeded in driving German troops from the Rhineland. Instead, it would certainly have escalated into a general European war; and, in March 1936, neither the governments nor the people of France and Britain considered the Rhineland worth a world war. Not only was the Rhineland German territory, but, in both nations, there were powerful elements sympathetic to Germany, elements that regarded Hitler as a bulwark against communism, and that believed Hitler's activities were simply accomplishing the much-needed revision of the Treaty of Versailles. Because German troops had not violated the French and Belgian frontiers, world opinion would have condemned Britain and France for their invasion of Germany in the same way that world opinion would condemn the military intervention of the United States in Vietnam thirty years later.

THE POPULAR FRONT AND THE SPANISH CIVIL WAR

As Europe adjusted to the new German power, a fresh political coalition formed in opposition to nazism and fascism appeared to offer hope. Shortly after the signing of the Franco-Soviet Pact, Georgi Dimitrov, Secretary-General of the Communist International, issued orders for all Communist parties to combine with bourgeois democratic parties in a broad Popular Front against fascism. Suddenly, Communist parties everywhere discovered their historical ties with bourgeois democracy. In the United States, American Communists aped the Daughters of the American Revolution by proclaiming their patriotism and their love of Lincoln and Washington. French Communists swore their devotion to the Revolution of 1789. Fearful of suffering the fate of their German comrades, the French Communists utilized the idea of the Popular Front in 1934, successfully making overtures to the Socialists and Radical Socialists to unite with them.

The Communist parties, by opposing fascism and allying themselves with non-Fascist parties, achieved a much needed popularity, which helped to attract new members. But the Popular Front failed to halt fascism, chiefly because the Communists never sincerely supported bourgeois democracy. Although they publicly appeared to back the Popular Front, they did not stop their efforts at undermining and destroying the Socialist and Democratic parties.

Despite the failure of the Popular Front to defeat fascism, it was successful in duping a large number of people into believing that Stalin was eager to protect bourgeois democracy. However, Stalin had sworn to destroy western capitalism, and he would never willingly have defended it unless he needed it for his own ends. At the time the Popular Front developed, Stalin had begun a purge of his opposition. Knowing that this ordeal would weaken Soviet defenses, Stalin needed some kind of temporary protection. The Popular Front seemed to offer that protection by arousing the West against Germany, by keeping alive resistance to nazism, and by distracting Hitler. Furthermore, the Popular Front could prove so annoying to Hitler that he might be willing to resume ties with Soviet Russia—ties that Stalin wanted.

For the purpose of maintaining the illusion of cooperation with the West, Stalin sent Maxim Litvinov to the League of Nations as his spokesman, to preach sermons on the virtues of collective security. If the western democracies, by practicing collective security, could keep Hitler occupied and away from Russia, Stalin could have the opportunity to destroy his critics, many of whom opposed collaboration with Hitler. Stalin would support the idea of collective security and the Popular Front as long as he could profit from the sacrifices of western nations, but he had no intention of allowing Russian soldiers to invade Germany to protect the capitalists.

The most glorious moment for the Popular Front came during the Spanish Civil War. In July 1936, the legally elected Popular Front government was attacked by rebels led by General Francisco Franco. To defeat the Popular Front, Franco called on Hitler and Mussolini for aid. Both men were delighted at being needed and courted. Hitler sent aid to the Spanish rebels, not for the benefit of Spain, but for the profit of Germany. A Spanish ally could further hinder the French, obliging them to divide their forces between two fronts, and could interfere with British naval communications in the Mediterranean. In addition, a prolonged civil war in Spain would distract foreign attention from Germany and its growing armaments while Hitler pursued his expansionist policies in eastern Europe. A Spanish government sympathetic to Nazi Germany could also be persuaded to provide submarine bases with access to the Mediterranean and Atlantic. However, Hitler did not have a long-range scheme for changing Spain into a Nazi state. He certainly did not plan to commit Germany to full-scale war in Spain. He simply found the situation advantageous for the moment.

In the early weeks of the conflict, Hitler saved the rebel cause by dispatching transport planes to ferry Franco's troops from North Africa. Before the war ended in 1939—with a rebel victory—over 16,000 German soldiers, airmen, and civilians had served in Spain. Not only did their efforts help bring Franco his victory, but they also provided the Luftwaffe with a laboratory to test planes and bombs that would later serve Hitler well against Poland, Britain, and France.

Mussolini also seized the chance offered by Franco, hoping to expand his sphere of influence in the Mediterranean. He lent his assistance with the expectation that Franco's Spain would be a satellite Fascist state. Furthermore, Fascist victory in Spain would compel France to concentrate fewer troops along the Italian frontier. Also, the invitation to display the prowess of his soldiers and airmen was too great an opportunity for Mussolini to pass up. To secure the support of the Roman Catholic Church in his venture, he maintained publicly that Italy was fighting to prevent the establishment of a Communist government in Spain. Finally, the joint intervention of Italy and Germany in the Spanish Civil War helped lay the foundation for a later alliance with Hitler.

Despite the intervention of German and Italian forces in the Spanish Civil War, Stalin hesitated before aiding the hard-pressed Popular Front government. Although he belatedly committed the Soviet Union to the cause of the Republic, he did not relish the expense, and he never dispatched enough aid to bring victory. Like a bourgeois capitalist, Stalin was willing only to sell Russian aid for Spanish gold and raw materials, and he deliberately limited the use of the aid—there were never more than

2,000 Russian citizens in Spain, and they had orders to remain out of artillery range. Later, all of those Russians who served in Spain were purged from the Soviet hierarchy because they had been affected so strongly by the liberal idealism of those men and women who battled Franco's legions, and this kind of idealism was too dangerous for Stalin's regime.

By keeping the war going without achieving victory, Stalin hoped that Britain and France would eventually intervene in Spain, thereby occupying Hitler with a western war. Such a conflict—under the terms of the Franco-Soviet pact—would in no way obligate Russia to battle Germany on behalf of France. For Stalin preferred that others support the Loyalist cause and fight the war, so that he could demonstrate his potential worth to Hitler with whom he desired an understanding over Central Europe.

But Britain and France did not see their policy quite as Stalin wanted them to. In Britain, Conservative opinion regarded Franco as the symbol of order and efficiency. British businessmen, with extensive interests in Spain, believed they would fare better with Franco than with the Popular Front. Both Conservative and Labor parties were divided internally over the Spanish Civil War, but all factions were opposed to direct involvement in the war—although some Laborites recommended aid to the Loyalists toward the end of the conflict. When aid from the Soviet Union gave the impression that the Loyalists were Communists, Roman Catholic opinion swung to Franco. From the beginning of the fighting, the British government insisted on localizing the conflict lest it spread beyond Spain, igniting a larger war.

In France, amid a wave of sit-down strikes that paralyzed the economy, a new government had taken office. Because the new government was the French equivalent of the Popular Front —an unstable coalition of Socialists, Radical-Socialists, and Communists—and because of the geographical proximity between Spain and France, it was natural for the Loyalists to ask France for aid. Sympathetic to the Loyalists, Leon Blum, the Socialist intellectual leader of the coalition, at first agreed to the sale of arms. However, the British government pressured him to change his mind. After more deliberations in Paris and London, the Blum cabinet finally stopped the sale of war materials to Spain. Although London's attitude had influenced this decision to a certain degree, French public opinion had been more powerful. The Radical-Socialists refused to support aid to the Spanish Republican forces; and their departure from the Popular Front would have wrecked the cabinet, thereby ending Blum's hopes for extensive social legislation. Additional opposition came from French Rightists, who viewed the war as a struggle between communism and Christianity and hoped that a Franco victory would regenerate France after bringing down the Popular Front government. It was this intense opposition to the Spanish government that convinced Blum that he would be risking civil war if he sold munitions to the Loyalists.

Blum accepted a plan for an international non-intervention agreement that had originated in the French Foreign Ministry. Convinced that he was saving France from civil war as well as protecting Europe from a general conflict, he proposed the plan to European foreign ministries. Germany, Italy, and the Soviet Union were among the nations that signed the agreement forbidding not only the export of war materials to Spain but all interference in the war. Although an international committee was established to supervise the agreement, Germany, Italy, and Russia violated their pledges; and, despite these infractions, London and Paris persisted in the farce of non-intervention, preventing aid to the Loyalist cause, aiding Franco and prolonging the civil war.

Reports of the horrors inflicted on the civilian population by the warring factions gave added strength to those who urged appeasement as a means of avoiding a similar struggle throughout Europe. The German and Italian air assaults on poorly defended Spanish cities appeared to be rehearsals for similar attacks on London and Paris. Because the Spanish cities were reduced to rubble in only a few days of bombing, the French and English were able to envision the destruction of their own vulnerable cities. These fears, implanted here, would be harvested during the Munich crisis in 1938.

For all those who believed the right place to fight fascism was on the battlefield, the Spanish Civil War became a crusade. British left-wing intellectuals and workingmen, German and Italian exiles, World War I veterans, unemployed Frenchmen, assorted Communists, and American idealists flocked to join the International Brigades, convinced that they were fighting for democracy. They died believing that, by defeating Franco, they would strike at Hitler; but even if Franco had been defeated, neither nazism nor Hitler's rule would have disappeared. Actually, a defeat would have had very little effect on Hitler, for Spain had never concerned him as anything more than a means of distracting European attention from Germany. Like Stalin, he had supplied only enough help to keep the war in progress. Finally, in 1939, when he no longer needed the distraction, and when he was certain that France and Britain would not attempt to stop him if he escalated the war, he dispatched enough help to give victory to Franco.

Should France and Britain have gone to war in 1936 in an attempt to defeat fascism in Spain, would it have made any difference in the eventual outcome of World War II? Probably not. Because of the deep divisions within these countries, a major war over Spain at that time would not have proved more favorable for them than the major war over Poland was to be in 1939. However favorable or unfavorable war might have been, it was extremely unlikely that Britain and France could have involved themselves in such a conflict. Their governments did not believe that the Spanish Civil War endangered their national security enough to justify the risk. The accuracy of their judgment was revealed during World War II when Franco was more of an inconvenience to the Allies than a direct threat. Franco even double-crossed his benefactors, Hitler and Mussolini, when they tried to cash their promissory notes. In 1940, after France had fallen, Franco scorned their pleas to help them against Britain.

Despite the reluctance of the British and French governments to involve their countries in Spain, the Spanish Civil War did influence their policies. Because it appeared to be a rehearsal for a European conflict, it frightened London and Paris into a more frantic search for ways to appease the aggressors. It also reinforced the arguments of the appeasers that nothing must be left undone that might prevent another world war.

APPEASEMENT AND APPEASERS

Since 1945, the word "appeasement" has become a derogatory term to be hurled at any statesman willing to negotiate with an opponent. However, at one time, it was a term applied to a policy that was not only publicly approved, but also praised. While appeasement has most often been associated with Neville Chamberlain, he did not actually originate the policy, but inherited it from his predecessors. It was not a policy created suddenly in the 1930s to buy off Hitler and Mussolini. It had originated in the minds of Englishmen who believed that World War I need never have come and that the outbreak of the war was entirely accidental. These Englishmen believed that both Britain and Germany shared responsibility for the outbreak of the war—an idea nurtured by revisionist historians who argued that the Treaty of Versailles was unjust and should be revised.

But appeasement also stemmed from a lack of faith in the British cause in World War I and from a firm resolve to prevent Europe from accidentally becoming entangled in another world war. Englishmen who looked with favor on the German educational system, on German industrial development, and on German social legislation became appeasement-minded. There was no one man or group of men who can be considered responsible for appeasement. Rather, a combination of forces—the horrors of the trenches, the disillusionment over the Treaty of Versailles, and the reluctance to burden Germany with total responsibility for the war—generated and fostered the policy.

Their guilt feelings over the Treaty of Versailles inclined the appeasers to take a soft line whenever Germany complained about the severity of the treaty restrictions. In the early 1920s, French insistence on complete fulfillment of the Versailles treaty alarmed the appeasers who feared that France would force Germany to take up arms again. Consequently, they argued that war could be prevented only by non-fulfillment of the treaty terms.

British opposition to the French occupation of the Ruhr in 1923–1924 had the effect of preventing the enforcement of the Treaty of Versailles. At the same time, it rescued Germany from being torn apart by the separatist movements that had begun to develop. When French troops withdrew from the Rhineland, the appeasers, as well as the Germans, had won a great victory; if France could not enforce the treaty, then it would never be enforced, and without enforcement, revision of the treaty—the appeasers' goal—would be easier.

J. Ramsey MacDonald, who became Prime Minister in 1924, helped clear up the difficulty that resulted from the Ruhr occupation by pushing the Dawes Plan through to completion. Under his leadership, a conference in London in the summer of 1924 brought Frenchmen and Germans together to consider the reparations problem. The nations who met at the London Conference agreed to end the Ruhr occupation and to assist German recovery with a loan—but they refused to help France and Belgium, both of whom had suffered heavier damage than had Germany. With these concessions granted, Germany agreed to pay the reparations at a reduced rate. Because Britain and its allies treated the former enemy as an equal, appeasement became more firmly established.

Stanley Baldwin, who in 1924 succeeded MacDonald as Prime Minister, was well-acquainted with the habits of the British electorate, but he paid as little attention as possible to foreign affairs, preferring to postpone unpopular decisions on the chance that they would solve themselves. Truly ignorant of foreign affairs and socially uneasy with foreigners, he could neither comprehend nor deal with the impending conflict in Europe, and so resolved on peace at any price. He was well aware of the German breaches in the Treaty of Versailles, but he unhesitatingly accepted the Locarno Pact. It did seem at the time that the final solution to Europe's postwar problems had been reached at Locarno. Many of the appeasers envisioned the treaty as creating a new spirit that would bring peace to Europe. Because Germany had freely participated in a conference and had willingly signed an agreement, the appeasers were convinced that they had replaced the ineffective Treaty of Versailles with an agreement that could be maintained.

When Hitler came to power, the arguments in favor of appeasement increased. Whatever faults the new Germany might possess, the appeasers believed that it could not have been as great a threat as the threat of Communist Russia. And, as long as the new Germany was not Communist, it could serve as a barrier to Russia. They believed that German rearmament should be accepted and changes must be made in the Treaty of Versailles.

By 1937, when Neville Chamberlain became Prime Minister, appeasement had become entrenched as British foreign policy. He was not a naive man as many would want to paint him, but actually a seasoned politician. Son of the famous Joseph Chamberlain, Neville had trained for a career in business. He understood contracts, accounts, and production schedules better than the intricacies of European diplomacy. He was conscientious but lacking in imagination; and his brusque and obstinate manner did not gain him popularity. Convinced that the techniques of business would succeed in international diplomacy, Chamberlain approached Hitler and Mussolini as he would a fellow businessman, offering them deals that would be mutually advantageous.

Distrustful of career men in the Foreign Office, he relied too much on his narrow background and on men whose grasp of European affairs was minimal. Men such as Hoare, Simon, Halifax, and Wilson were poor choices for advisors. Both Hoare and Simon had been failures at formulating foreign policy, and Halifax's ignorance of European affairs had made him ill-prepared to be Foreign Secretary. The last member of the quartet, Sir Horace Wilson, was a very capable civil servant, an expert in labor disputes with the title of "Chief Industrial Adviser to the Government," but in foreign affairs he was strictly an amateur. Given an office in No. 10 Downing Street, he acted unofficially for Chamberlain, often presenting his views in behind-the-scenes meetings with German officials.

Chamberlain would not listen to Eden, the Foreign Secretary he had inherited from the Baldwin cabinet. The Prime Minister believed that diplomats wasted time in red tape, and that he must handle his own foreign policy in order to avoid this problem. When he took office, he had resolved to end the policy of drift and inaction that had typified the Baldwin administration; and to do this, he believed he had to act quickly and independently on policy matters. It was to be expected that he would clash with Eden, who preferred more traditional ways of dealing with the Fascist powers.

The difficulties between Chamberlain and Eden came into the open over a proposal made by Franklin Roosevelt that the diplomatic corps in Washington meet to consider an agreement on the basic principles of international conduct. This agreement would include decisions on the reduction of armaments, methods of promoting economic security, and measures for protecting neutrals in wartime. Chamberlain objected strenuously to this plan; he was certain that it would not only fail but also ruin all his efforts at appeasement. Without informing Eden of his move, Chamberlain requested Roosevelt to postpone putting his plan into effect. Eden, who thought he saw excellent possibilities in the Roosevelt proposal, had no success in convincing Chamberlain to change his mind. Although he has generally been condemned for rejecting the President's impractical scheme, Chamberlain, because of Roosevelt's previous unwillingness to commit the United States to any international responsibility, had some justification in believing the efforts would come to naught. The only important result of Roosevelt's proposal was to strain the relations between Chamberlain and Eden to the breaking point.

The breaking point came almost immediately—on the question of Ethiopia. In hopes of separating Mussolini from Hitler, Chamberlain wanted immediate discussions over recognition of the Italian conquest of Ethiopia. Eden preferred to negotiate on a *quid pro quo* basis: Mussolini could withdraw his troops from Spain, and then Britain would recognize the conquest of Ethiopia. When Chamberlain rejected Eden's recommendation entirely, the Foreign Secretary resigned.

Edward, third Viscount Halifax, who followed Eden as Foreign Secretary, was much more to Chamberlain's liking. A country gentleman, a former Viceroy of India, and a High-Church Anglican with deep spiritual convictions, Halifax was completely unsuspecting when confronted with men such as Hitler and Mussolini. He had never bothered to read *Mein Kampf,* and he believed that the men who had warned against Hitler were exaggerating. But this was the man whom Chamberlain wanted as Foreign Secretary—a faithful servant of the King who would not object to whatever brand of appeasement Chamberlain wanted to practice.

Before he took office, and despite the protests of Eden, Halifax was sent on his first errand for Chamberlain. In November 1937, Halifax accepted an invitation from Hermann Goering to attend the Sporting Exhibition in Berlin. On November 17, the English country gentleman met with Hitler at Berchtesgaden; but he almost wrecked the meeting at the outset by mistaking Hitler for a footman, stopping short of handing the dictator his hat. Halifax was in agreement with Hitler on the inequity of the Treaty of Versailles, but he wanted the potentially dangerous questions arising from the treaty—Danzig, Austria, Czechoslovakia—handled in a peaceful way. He promised that the British government would not "block reasonable settlements . . . reached with the free assent and goodwill of those primarily concerned." [4] This was just short of an invitation for Hitler to do whatever he wanted in Central Europe. Hitler had already—in the Reichschancellery meeting—announced plans for expansion; but now, thanks to Halifax (and Chamberlain), he had the means for taking the territory he wanted. If he could make his moves appear to be in accordance with the wishes of the people in the territories occupied, he would have British consent.

The policy that resulted in this invitation to Hitler had developed considerably since Versailles. In retrospect, appeasement had so managed to root itself into British foreign policy as to make it extremely difficult—if not impossible for Chamberlain to have taken any other approach. Under Lloyd George, with his attempts to make Wilson lighten the Treaty of Versailles, appeasement became the keystone of British foreign policy. All of Lloyd George's successors followed his example: Andrew Bonar Law denounced the French occupation of the Ruhr in 1923; MacDonald, in his first administration, got the French out of the Ruhr, and in his second administration, preached disarmament of Britain and its allies as a means of satisfying German complaints about military inequities; and Baldwin aided the growth of appeasement by making the Anglo-German Naval Agreement the crowning diplomatic achievement of his third government.

By the time Chamberlain came to office in 1937, appeasement would no longer satisfy Hitler (whom Chamberlain regarded as a German politician with strong feelings about the Versailles treaty and the suffering German people). Nevertheless, Chamberlain prescribed a more vigorous form of appease-

[4] Lord Birkenhead, *Halifax* (London, 1966), p. 370.

ment than had his predecessors, pushing for intensive discussions and, if necessary, face-to-face negotiations between heads of state. Appeasement to Chamberlain did not mean surrendering to Hitler's demands, however, but it meant finding ways of satisfying those demands by wise concessions that would avoid further dangers to peace. Chamberlain honestly believed that world peace could be guaranteed by economic prosperity, by ending existing economic difficulties; and he believed that these troubles could be solved by reducing military expenditures and by balancing national budgets. Germany, he believed, would become more peacefully inclined if southeastern Europe were opened to German economic exploitation, thereby ridding the country of the need for a massive army and providing the German economy with a market. This fact has often been minimized in evaluating the years before the war. For Chamberlain practiced appeasement, not out of cowardice or fear, but out of a positive belief that appeasement would open the way to peace for all.

Chamberlain did not deliberately appease Hitler in order to turn his aggressive activities away from the West and toward the Soviet Union—Chamberlain was not as cunning as that. True, he distrusted the Russians, but he believed that another world war would devastate Europe and leave Communists in control. To Chamberlain as well as the other appeasers, the greatest evil of all—the evil to be avoided at all costs—was war. One world war was sufficient to make the appeasers fearful of what the outcome of such a major conflict might be.

The appeasers did ignore one important fact: a policy of appeasement could end only with Germany restored to its former strength. Given the German population, industry, educational system, and—above all—geographical position, appeasement must result in German domination of Central Europe and perhaps in an attempt to dominate all of the Continent as well. The appeasers' sins were the sins of all of the post-1919 generation, who read Keynes, regretted the Treaty of Versailles, sorrowed for Germany, and admired Mussolini for running trains on time. They took too optimistic a view of the Germans, always conceding the benefit of the doubt in hopes of bringing peace. Through improved Anglo-German relations, they sought to avoid direct conflict. Although they would later be reviled for their actions, the appeasers did perform a vital task: their efforts for peace proved without a doubt that Hitler could not be trusted and eventually convinced Britain that war was necessary and just.

4 / The Road to War, 1938

THE REICHSCHANCELLERY MEETING

On November 5, 1937, Hitler summoned a select group of ministers and military leaders to a meeting in the Reichschancellery. In the history of Nazi Germany, this meeting has come to have a great deal of significance because it seems to have indicated deliberate planning for another world war. If Hitler had plans for European conquest, his staff needed to be informed, for they were not simply party hacks but included Hermann Goering, Commander-in-Chief of the Luftwaffe; General Werner von Fritsch, Commander-in-Chief of the army; Constantine von Neurath, Foreign Minister; Field Marshal Werner von Blomberg, Minister of War; Admiral Eric Raeder, Commander-in-Chief of the navy; and Colonel Friedrich Hossbach, Hitler's military adjutant. Hossbach has contributed to our knowledge of this meeting by making an unofficial record reconstructed from notes made during the meeting. Hitler called the conference because of a quarrel among his staff: Blomberg had complained about Goering's rapacity in acquiring raw materials for the air force. Hitler found it necessary to expound his goals to prevent these quarrels from hindering the preparations of the armed forces for German aggrandizement.

To impress his audience, Hitler announced that his words

were to be considered his last will and testament. He asserted that the problem of German living space had become a crisis; complete self-sufficiency would not supply all Germany's needs for raw materials and food. He insisted that the solution to this problem lay in acquiring living space in the countries surrounding Germany. Because rearmament was nearly complete and any delay in solving the problem of living space would mean greater obsolescence in equipment, Germany must take the offensive before other nations finished rearming. Each year the nation's leaders would grow older, and the Nazi party would lose its momentum, while the threat of a lower standard of living would increase as the population continued to grow. Asserting that he had no choice but to act, Hitler vowed to solve Germany's problem of living space no later than 1943–1945.

For his *Lebensraum,* he looked to the south and the east. The incorporation of Czechoslovakia and Austria into Germany, Hitler argued, would provide the Fatherland with a more defensible frontier and with new sources of manpower, raw materials, and food. Further, if France should continue to be embroiled in internal problems, Germany could move against Czechoslovakia, and it seemed likely that Britain would not permit France to attack Germany. But if Germany should become involved in a war with Britain and France, Czechoslovakia and Austria would have to be overthrown simultaneously to protect the eastern flank. Once Czechoslovakia had been defeated, Hitler expected, Poland would be passive.

However, Hitler firmly believed that Britain and France had already written off Czechoslovakia and that neither Italy nor Russia would be sufficiently concerned to intervene. He brazenly predicted that, in any case, France would be unable to act against Germany because, by the summer of 1938, both France and England would be too busy fighting with Italy in Spain. Consequently it would be in Germany's interest for the Spanish Civil War to continue.

Hitler's pronouncements provoked sharp questioning from

Fritsch and Blomberg, who opposed taking any action that might place Britain and France in the position of becoming Germany's enemies. Hitler retorted that under no circumstances would Britain be likely to join in a war against Germany; and, without British backing, they could be assured that France would be afraid to take any action. But the generals warned that, should there be such a conflict, Germany would not be entirely in the clear, because France would still possess sufficient troops to have superiority on the western front. Blomberg argued that mobilization in France had proceeded further than it had in Germany, that the western German defenses were inadequate, and that the motorized divisions of the German army would not be able to fulfill the tasks they would be given. Blomberg also worried over the strength of the Czechoslovak fortifications, which had been modeled on the Maginot Line. This problem was so important, Fritsch contended, that he had already ordered a special study of methods to breach these fortifications. He proposed to cancel his leave, which he had planned to spend abroad, but Hitler assured him that war was not imminent. Neurath expressed doubt that an Anglo-French–Italian conflict, predicted by Hitler, would be likely to break out so soon. Hitler stood by his assertion that war seemed possible in the summer of 1938. When these hostilities commenced, he wanted German forces to attack Czechoslovakia. According to Hossbach's memorandum, the argument subsided with the remainder of the conference devoted to a discussion of the armaments and raw materials problems, which had been the original excuse for the conference.

In assessing the significance of this conference, Hitler's remarks must not be dismissed simply because his predictions about the Spanish Civil War proved inaccurate. Hitler was neither daydreaming nor attempting to fool his audience. He knew he could accomplish little without their cooperation. He was neither prophesying nor planning, but was describing opportunities that Germany should be ready to exploit. He had confessed to his audience that he no longer would limit his actions to ending restrictions remaining in the Versailles treaty, but instead would seize lands never ruled by the Hohenzollerns. His goal now was conquest, not treaty revision.

However, the conference also proved to have served another purpose, for three of the audience—Fritsch, Blomberg, and Neurath—were soon relieved of their positions. These three men had dared to question the feasibility of Hitler's ambitions, and they were forced to pay for their doubts. They had spoken up at this time only because Hitler had finally come into the open and spoken of cases, countries, and dates. They had gone along with Hitler before, because his earlier talks had been more obscure and indefinite.

Blomberg, evidently more disposed towards obeying his Fuehrer than were the others, obediently took steps to implement the new goals, but this did little to ward off his dismissal. He, like Fritsch—who tried unsuccessfully on November 9 to convince Hitler that his goals were impossible—and Neurath, would eventually have to atone for this lack of faith. He had his staff issue a new directive, dated December 7, 1937, to alter an earlier strategic plan known as *Operation Green,* which had been intended for a war on two fronts with the emphasis on the southeast. Although new plans had to be worked out for Hitler's offensive war, *Operation Green* would be used in case a favorable situation should develop in the meantime. It called for German armed forces to occupy Bohemia and Moravia speedily, leaving only a minimum force for security in the west. A surprise attack would be launched before the Czechoslovak forces mobilized, and the bulk of the Luftwaffe would be committed against Czechoslovakia.

Those who drafted the directive had grasped the meaning of the Reichschancellery conference: Czechoslovakia would be the first target because potentially it was stronger than Austria. Yet when Hitler was presented with the opportunity, he would take Austria first.

On January 22, 1938, in a long speech to the senior officers, in which he wandered from one topic to another, Hitler eventually got around to his favorite theme—living space. He was still determined to convince his senior generals that his goals had to be fulfilled. In view of the growing German population, the food situation had become even more serious than he had originally thought. The only solution to this problem, he suggested, would be for Germany to take advantage of the common bond of race and language in Central Europe. But, because Hitler rambled from one topic to another, he lost the attention of his audience, and he interpreted the negative reaction to his speech as a lack of confidence in him.

His own confidence in the generals shaken, Hitler was now resolved to purge the High Command. Although Blomberg had willingly converted his program, Hitler felt that the Minister of War was inclined to panic. Therefore, he had to go. Blomberg made Hitler's task easy for him; on January 12, with Hitler and Goering as witnesses, Blomberg had married Erna Gruhn, a typist who had formerly been a prostitute. To save the honor of the German officer corps when this information was revealed, Blomberg was forced to resign. Ordinarily his successor would have been Fritsch, but because Fritsch had a tough mind and looked down on the Nazis with conservative distaste, the Fuehrer could not allow him to become the Minister of War. This problem was solved by Goering and Himmler, who confronted Fritsch with a trumped-up charge of homosexuality, prompting his resignation.

General Walther von Brauchitsch, an admirer of Hitler, succeeded Fritsch as Commander-in-Chief of the army, and Hitler became his own Minister of War. He announced these changes on February 4, retired a number of generals found wanting in their devotion, and replaced Neurath with Joachim von Ribbentrop.

This purge gave Hitler greater control over those areas vital to securing the objectives he had discussed in the Reichschancellery meeting. He had succeeded in ridding himself of those men in high office from whom opposition could be anticipated, and he had replaced them with men who were both acquainted with and prepared for the route Hitler was traveling.

THE ANSCHLUSS

Although Czechoslovakia was supposed to be the main target according to Hitler's Reichschancellery pronouncement and the Wehrmacht directive of December 7, the opportunity to take Austria occurred first. A desire for *Anschluss* (union of Germany and Austria) had created controversy in the years since 1918. As early as the closing months of World War I, when the Imperial German armies were retreating before the advancing Allied forces, General Erich Ludendorff pressed the Foreign Ministry to seek *Anschluss* to soften the sting of defeat, but the more responsible ministers refused to endanger the delicate peace negotiations with such a provocative act. Envisioning such a threat, Clemenceau insisted on inclusion of Article 80 in the Versailles treaty, prohibiting *Anschluss* unless approved by the Council of the League of Nations.

During the 1920s, the feeling for union between the two countries was stronger in Austria than in Germany. Agitation in certain Austrian areas led to unofficial plebiscites, which carried overwhelmingly in favor of *Anschluss*. Although the Versailles powers eventually found it necessary to order the cessation of these movements, by 1930, the depression had stirred up Austrian sentiment for *Anschluss* as the way to revive the economy. At this time, the government in Berlin was desperate for some foreign policy victory to counter the growing Nazi accusations that the Weimar Republic had given in too easily at Versailles.

On March 21, 1931, after secret discussions, the Austrian and German governments suddenly announced that they had agreed on a projected customs union, which would remove all trade barriers between Austria and Germany and create an economic *Anschluss*. Because they had feared opposition, the two governments had not discussed the plan with other governments before making the public announcement, as was customary in cases of agreement that might alter the balance of power. Apprehensive that these new economic ties might ultimately lead to complete *Anschluss*, the western powers, under French prodding, protested vehemently. France forced Austria to withdraw from the scheme by threatening to block a vitally needed loan. Because of the collapse of the Kreditanstalt, liquid capital was sorely needed in Vienna; and so, Austria gave in.

The World Court had the final word in the matter in September 1931, when it held that the customs union endangered the economic independence of Austria. The defeat of the customs union deprived the Weimar Republic of a sorely needed triumph over the Versailles powers to offset the growing strength of the Nazis. But the opponents of *Anschluss* were correct in assuming that it was not the answer to the economic needs of Germany and Austria. What was needed in Europe then was a Common Market, but this was too radical a solution for the time.

The *Anschluss* movement was renewed when Hitler came to power. The Fuehrer had never concealed his sentiments on the matter. They were spelled out clearly on the first page of *Mein Kampf*, and he never retracted his statements. He gave the incorporation of Austria into the greater Nazi Germany a prominent place in his program; and within Austria, he was aided by an active Nazi party that lived only for the day when Austria would be able to join the Third Reich.

After the debacle of July 1934, Hitler had to alter his tactics. Instead of depending on a successful coup by the Austrian Nazis, the Fuehrer had to try diplomacy to achieve *Anschluss*. He dispatched Franz von Papen to Vienna as the German minister with orders to patch up relations with Austria and to promote *Anschluss*. After prolonged negotiations, Papen convinced Austrian Chancellor Kurt von Schuschnigg to accept an Austro-

German agreement. Because there was no alternative, on July 11, 1936, Schuschnigg signed. Austria had possessed no allies who would come to its aid against an economically and militarily powerful Germany. Hoping that the agreement would ease tension between the two countries and lift part of the burden on Austrian economy, Schuschnigg accepted the German demands.

The published text of this agreement seemed innocent; but it actually represented capitulation of Austria to Hitler. Germany recognized the full sovereignty of the Austrian government, both countries pledged non-interference in the internal affairs of the other, and Austria acknowledged that it was a German state; but the real agreement, which contained a great many advantages for Germany and few for Austria, was kept secret. According to this document, Austrian Nazis would be free from harm as long as they complied with the laws of Austria. Both Germany and Austria renounced the use of radio, motion pictures, newspapers, and the theater for propaganda purposes. Both countries removed all restrictions on the sale of books from the other country. Five newspapers from each nation would be permitted circulation within the other. Germany promised to lift economic restrictions on trade as well as tourism—a concession important to Austria. Schuschnigg agreed to conduct Austrian foreign policy to conform to the policies of Germany and to grant political amnesty to imprisoned Austrian Nazis. Finally, and most significantly, he promised to invite leaders of the opposition (Nazis or those sympathetic to nazism) to join his movement. The agreement of July 11, devised to achieve *Anschluss* by evolution, was like a leash tightened by Berlin slowly strangling Austrian independence. Although hidden from the rest of the world, the agreement was divulged to the Austrian Nazi leaders, who were ordered by Hitler on July 16 "to work for the *Anschluss* through the July 11 Agreement." [1]

In operation, the agreement proved to be quite detrimental

[1] Friedrich Rainer testimony, *Trials of the Major War Criminals* (Nuremberg, 1946), XVI, p. 124.

to Austria. The newspapers and books from Germany were crammed with Nazi propaganda critical of the Austrian government, and any Austrian censorship of these publications would violate the July agreement. If the Vienna government dared to enforce the civil laws against Austrian Nazis, Berlin would accuse Schuschnigg of violating the agreement. To comply with the agreement, Schuschnigg had to admit friends of the Nazis into his government, so he appointed Odo Neustaedter-Stuermer and Edmund Glaise-Horstenau. In 1937, Schuschnigg appointed Arthur Seyss-Inquart, whom he thought he could trust to be fairly moderate, but Seyss-Inquart was soon in communication with German officials and became the leader of those Austrian Nazis who sought a peaceful union with Germany.

Despite the agreement, Austro-German relations continued to deteriorate. On May 2, 1937, when the Austrian police raided the headquarters of the Nazi party in Vienna, they found material indicating collaboration between the German and Austrian Nazi parties. There were records of talks between Austrian Nazi leaders and Hitler, propaganda hostile to the Austrian government, evidence that the German government supplied funds to Austrian Nazis, and records of a courier service between the Austrian and German Nazi organizations. When confronted with this subversion, Papen responded by attacking Schuschnigg for exhausting Hitler's patience by his failure to keep the agreement.

When Hitler discussed Austria at the Reichschancellery meeting on November 5, 1937, it is significant that he no longer talked about an evolutionary policy for *Anschluss* but actually spoke of "attacking" Austria. Although Hitler feared Czechoslovakia more than he feared Austria at this date, because of a combination of chance and human error, Austria would prove to be the first nation his forces would occupy. Another raid on the Austrian Nazi party headquarters in Vienna on January 25, 1938 uncovered plans for a Nazi coup, but Schuschnigg refused to publish these documents because he feared that they might antagonize Hitler. According to the plans, Austrian Nazis, by resorting to riots and acts of sabotage, would provoke the Austrian government into deploying troops to restore law and order. Berlin would then send an ultimatum demanding the withdrawal of the troops and the incorporation of the Nazis into the Austrian government; once inside the government, they could then begin the take-over. If the Schuschnigg government rejected the ultimatum, it would be violating the July 11 agreement, and Hitler would have an excuse for an invasion. It is uncertain whether Hitler knew of the existence of these plans; but, had the coup come about and presented him with a chance for *Anschluss,* there is no doubt that he would have seized it.

Despite the discovery of these plans, Schuschnigg continued his struggle to pacify the Nazis while trying to govern Austria, but it became more difficult daily. Hoping that a meeting with Hitler would help to calm the more militant Austrian Nazis, Schuschnigg, in early January 1938, accepted an invitation from Hitler for a meeting on January 26. However, because Hitler had become involved in the crisis over the army High Command, he postponed the meeting to mid-February. To create a favorable atmosphere for the meeting with Hitler, Schuschnigg commenced negotiating Austrian Nazi demands. But in the process of negotiating, he granted concessions he could ill afford. These included development of close military, economic, and political relations with Germany to be carried out with the help of Austrian Nazis. He also agreed to a reconstruction of the cabinet that would place Austrian Nazis in charge of some ministries.

In his purge of the German diplomatic corps, on February 5, Hitler recalled Papen. Schuschnigg took this to mean that more aggressive measures would follow. In a conference with Hitler, Papen revealed the extent of Schuschnigg's concessions. Involved in a struggle with the generals, the German dictator had forgotten the planned meeting with Schuschnigg until

Papen had reminded him. Hitler seized on a meeting with the Austrian chancellor as a chance to divert attention away from the turmoil within the German government. By forcing public concessions from Schuschnigg, Hitler would win a diplomatic victory that would offset the effects of the purge of the generals and the diplomats. Acting under instructions from Hitler, Papen returned to Vienna with another invitation for Schuschnigg to visit Hitler at Berchtesgaden on February 12 and with a promise that the July 11 agreement would be reaffirmed without any additional political demands. Hoping to improve Austro-German relations through the meeting, Schuschnigg accepted the invitation.

The meeting between Hitler and Schuschnigg took place at Berchtesgaden on February 12. Schuschnigg expected a dignified discussion between two statesmen, but he encountered a storm. Hitler accused him of hostility towards Germany: Austria should have left the League of Nations when Germany did, Hitler raved; instead of supporting Germany, Austria had committed high treason by remaining in the League. In his tirade, Hitler styled himself the greatest German in history and swore to fulfill his divine mission of resolving the Austrian question. If Schuschnigg should dare to oppose Hitler by ordering resistance, German troops would overrun Austrian defenses within half an hour. Neither Britain, France, nor Italy would intervene to thwart his plans; and he swore that he was not bluffing. Caught off guard by Hitler's assault, Schuschnigg apologized. Suddenly Hitler cut short his tirade for luncheon, which was accompanied by polite conversation about horses, motor cars, and such. Afterwards the host withdrew, leaving Schuschnigg and Austrian Foreign Minister Guido Schmidt alone with a few German generals who had been summoned there for the purpose of intimidating the Austrians.

While the victims waited, Hitler, Ribbentrop, and Papen prepared demands for further concessions based on those already granted earlier in Vienna. Then in mid-afternoon, they presented Schuschnigg with two typewritten pages containing the demands. Schuschnigg must promise to exchange views with Hitler on foreign policy and to assist Hitler's policies. The Austrian Nazi party could not be outlawed. Economic discrimination against Nazis, as well as discrimination against Austrian Nazis in the government and armed forces, must be ended. Schuschnigg must appoint Seyss-Inquart Minister of the Interior with special authority to oversee the activities of the Austrian Nazis; the position would also give him supervision of the police. A general amnesty must be proclaimed for Austrian Nazis who had been imprisoned for breaking the law; men sympathetic to the Nazis must be given important positions in the Austrian Press Bureau. Better relations between the German and Austrian armies would be fostered by conferences between the General Staffs and by an exchange of officers; the Austrian Chief of Staff should be replaced by a general who would be friendly to Germany. If Schuschnigg carried out these demands, Austria would be well on the way to becoming a German satellite.

Stunned, Schuschnigg protested: he had been promised only affirmation of the July 11 agreement, not a new set of demands. After the failure of Ribbentrop and Papen to persuade the Austrian Chancellor, Hitler summoned Schuschnigg for a fresh attack. He demanded that Schuschnigg sign the document or Germany would take action that very night. Schuschnigg refused, claiming that he lacked authority to sign such a document. Hitler stepped hurriedly to the door.

"General Keitel!" he shouted.

"I shall have you called later," he yelled at Schuschnigg.[2]

Keitel, the new chief of the High Command, entered quickly and Schuschnigg left the room. Because of Hitler's threats, Schuschnigg imagined the worst—Hitler must be giving Keitel orders for an attack. Actually Hitler was only bluffing but the agonizing minutes that passed had the desired effect on

[2] Kurt von Schuschnigg, *Austrian Requiem* (New York, 1946), p. 24.

Schuschnigg. Finally, when he reappeared, Hitler graciously offered to give Schuschnigg three days to accept the new demands. Confused, isolated, fearful of war, Schuschnigg gave in. When he returned to Vienna, Schuschnigg covered up the threat to Austrian independence because of rumors of German war preparations, which had been purposely instigated by Hitler shortly after Schuschnigg left Berchtesgaden. The French government, after learning a portion of the truth, expressed concern to Berlin and was in turn rebuffed. The British Foreign Office was helpless because of the struggle then going on between Eden and Chamberlain. Schuschnigg also sought advice from Mussolini, who recommended that he accept Hitler's demands. Forsaken by the Stresa powers—who had publicly sworn to uphold the independence of Austria—Schuschnigg yielded on February 15.

From Hitler's references to Austria in the weeks following the Berchtesgaden meeting, it is clear that he expected the February demands to complete the July agreement and accomplish *Anschluss*. As a result of those most recent concessions, the Austrian Nazis became bolder, and the police—thanks to Seyss-Inquart, the new Minister of the Interior—became more undependable. After a few feeble efforts to arouse the nation, Schuschnigg finally decided to seek support by means of a national plebiscite to be held on March 13. He hoped a favorable vote would unite the nation behind him, but he had already gone too far in transforming Austria into a German satellite. One plebiscite could not arouse sufficient resistance to *Anschluss*. Guns, tanks, and soldiers, not votes, were required to withstand German aggression.

However, if the plebiscite succeeded, it would be an immense propaganda victory for Schuschnigg. Thanks to a spy in an Austrian cabinet ministry, Hitler learned of the plebiscite before Schuschnigg announced it publicly. Infuriated, Hitler intervened. He ordered the generals commanding troops in the areas along the Austrian frontier to report to him early on the morning of March 10, and asked to be given the plans for invasion of Austria. But Keitel had to confess that there was only the barest sketch of a proposed study for an invasion of Austria, and that only in case of an attempted restoration of the Habsburg monarchy. Because there were other more pressing projects, and because Hitler had emphasized Czechoslovakia first, very little consideration had been given to Austria. Hitler ordered that plans be prepared quickly for an invasion of Austria, presumably to establish constitutional conditions and protect the Germans within Austria.

It was decided that the Eighth Army would march into Austria while the Luftwaffe would drop propaganda leaflets, occupy airfields, and lend support to the army. The troops were ordered to appear reluctant in taking action against their Austrian brethren. They should avoid bloodshed to give the operation the appearance of friendly troops being welcomed by the population. However, any resistance should be crushed. Hitler wished to appear peaceful for two reasons. He hoped to avoid resistance from sentimental Austrians who might be seduced by an appeal to their cultural ties with Germany. Further, if the occupation could be brought off peacefully, it would seem to western Europe to be nothing more than a reunion of the German peoples who had suffered so badly from the flaws of the Versailles treaty.

In the midst of all of this, there was one unknown element —Mussolini. Because his forces were tied down by the Spanish Civil War, he could not have prevented the *Anschluss* had he been so inclined. But, unless Hitler were sure of what his response would be, there was the possibility that he might cause trouble. Consequently, Hitler dispatched Prince Philip of Hesse, the son-in-law of the King of Italy, to Mussolini with a letter that "revealed" an Austro-Czechoslovak plot against Germany. The plot, which was pure fabrication, detailed how both countries were strengthening their borders and preparing for a restoration of the Habsburgs, an event that might require an attack on Germany. Schuschnigg, according to the letter, had broken his promise by scheduling a plebiscite with the intent of oppressing the people and engulfing Austria in anarchy. "In my responsibility as Fuehrer and Chancellor of the German Reich and likewise as a son of this soil," he wrote to Mussolini, "I can no longer remain passive in the face of these developments." [3] Law and order had to be restored in Austria in order to defend Germany. Hitler promised not to overstep the boundary into Italy; he would stop short of the Brenner Pass, and those Germans below the pass who might want to join the Reich would have to have their wishes unfulfilled. When Mussolini replied that he had already written off Austria, an ecstatic Hitler swore, "I will never forget, whatever may happen. If he should ever need any help or be in any danger, he can be convinced that I shall stick by him, whatever may happen, even if the whole world were against him." [4]

By 4:30 AM on March 11, German frontier officials had closed the Austrian borders. Later in the day, two Austrian ministers acting for Hitler brought Schuschnigg an ultimatum: postpone the plebiscite and arrange for a new one that would be slanted in favor of the Austrian Nazis or face armed German intervention. Arguments and conferences followed; and, in the afternoon, Schuschnigg called off the plebiscite, but Hitler would not let it go at that. Within half an hour, Goering telephoned an order for Schuschnigg and his government to resign. Seyss-Inquart, Schuschnigg's "friend," should form a new government. Schuschnigg was immediately ready to capitulate, but President Wilhelm Miklas refused to accept the new chancellor and, throughout the afternoon, searched for someone else to take on the burden of leading Austria in this crucial period.

During the afternoon, Schuschnigg asked the advice of the British government, but the reply was chilling: "His Majesty's

[3] Hitler to Mussolini, March 11, 1938, *Documents on German Foreign Policy*, Series D, I, p. 575.
[4] *Nazi Conspiracy and Aggression* (Washington, 1946), V, p. 642.

Government cannot take the responsibility of advising the Chancellor to take any course of action which might expose his country to dangers against which His Majesty's Government are unable to guarantee protection." [5] Nor could France offer help. The French cabinet had fallen on March 9; and now, as in the Rhineland crisis, a caretaker government was in office. Both Paris and London did make a halfhearted gesture toward consulting Mussolini on the subject, but when he received their suggestion rather coldly, they did not press the issue. Both governments made routine protests to the German Foreign Ministry, but these were simply for the record.

The attitude of the two western nations reinforced Schuschnigg's decision to resign. A peaceful surrender seemed the only alternative to a short bloody war that, he was certain, would result in the defeat of Austria. The Austrian forces could have delayed the German advance for only a few days at most because they had only about a two-day supply of ammunition, and the Austrian Nazis would have been certain to engage in rioting and sabotage to divert troops. Austria was clearly outmatched —its air force and anti-aircraft defenses were non-existent, and its tanks and artillery were few and old. Schuschnigg had no real choice but to reject the advice of those who begged him to attempt to block the German invasion.

Had anyone cared, Austrian resistance to the German invasion could have served as a warning to Europe, but the nations of Europe did not judge their vital interests to be at stake.

Late in the afternoon of March 11, Schuschnigg ordered the Austrian troops to withdraw from the frontier and to offer no resistance. Early in the evening, Schuschnigg's resignation was announced over the radio, and he went on the air later to announce that Austria would yield. In the streets of Vienna, the Nazis began to take control. Although German agents were already filtering into the Chancellery in Vienna, Seyss-Inquart had

[5] Halifax to Palairet, March 11, 1938, *Documents on British Foreign Policy,* Third Series, I, p. 13.

not yet become chancellor. About 8:30 PM Hitler decided it was necessary to launch the invasion. To give Hitler a "legal" excuse for the invasion, it was necessary for Goering, who had been keeping in touch with his agents in Vienna by telephone, to dictate a message to be wired to Berlin over Seyss-Inquart's signature calling for the entrance of German troops to prevent bloodshed and to restore law and order. In the early hours of March 12, Miklas gave in and Seyss-Inquart became chancellor.

When the German Eighth Army crossed into Austria later in the morning, they met no resistance. In the afternoon, Hitler himself entered Austria and received a joyous welcome from the citizens of Linz, where he had spent his boyhood. It was there that he came to his decision that a puppet government headed by Seyss-Inquart was a less desirable alternative than *Anschluss,* and, since occupation had been accomplished with no opposition and with only mild protestation from foreign governments, it could be achieved with little difficulty. During the crisis, Hitler had wavered in his opinion of how *Anschluss* should be achieved because he was uncertain of foreign reaction. With Danzig and the Polish Corridor, he would be able to claim to be retaking German territory unjustly ripped away by the Treaty of Versailles. But this was not the case with Austria. Also, the territory being violated by German troops was that of a member of the League of Nations, and there was a danger that the League members might take the action more seriously than they had Mussolini's rape of Ethiopia. Because the invasion of Austria meant going to the brink of war, Hitler had wavered, but his judgment of how Europe would react proved to be sound. The nations of Europe were just as relieved as Hitler when, on March 13, in compliance with Hitler's decision, the puppet government in Austria adopted a law declaring the country to be a province of the German Reich. Hitler's victory was sealed with a plebiscite on April 10, with over 99 percent of the Austrian voters approving the question, "Do you acknowledge Adolf Hitler as our Fuehrer and the reunion of Austria with the German Reich which was affected on March 11, 1938?" Many voted *ja* out of sheer relief that the uncertainty over Austria's future had ended.

However, this victory marked a change in Hitler's tactics. After this he would cease to concern himself simply with ending restrictions imposed on Germany by the Treaty of Versailles, and he would threaten independent nations with invasion, or even war, unless they capitulated to his demands. The results of his victory were impressive: without a shot being fired, without losing a soldier, and with only a few Austrian units mobilized, Germany had acquired 6½ million new citizens who would provide additional labor and manpower for eight new army divisions. The balance of power in Central Europe had been upset. With Germany now surrounding Czechoslovakia on three fronts, the Czechoslovak defenses were outflanked; and Yugoslavia, Italy, and Hungary were now confronted with German troops on their frontiers. Without the guns of the Wehrmacht being fired, one of the states that had emerged from the 1919 peace settlement had surrendered to German armies, and Hitler had won his first conquest in World War II.

CRISIS IN CZECHOSLOVAKIA

The successful *Anschluss* of Germany and Austria directly threatened the security of Czechoslovakia, whose defenses along the Austrian frontier had been allowed to weaken. Because the interests of Czechoslovakia were affected by the *Anschluss,* German officials took pains to inform the Prague government that the affair concerned only Germany and Austria and that Czechoslovakia should not be alarmed. But there was cause for alarm. Czechoslovakia contained the Sudeten Germans, a minority with dissatisfactions that could be exploited by Hitler to weaken the security of the country. Although Hitler actually had no interest in the grievances of the Sudeten Germans, he saw that they might be used to his advantage.

Scattered along the western frontiers of Czechoslovakia—in Bohemia and Moravia—were a large number of people whose ancestors had migrated from Germany. Although some had come as early as the twelfth century, they still considered themselves German in origin and culture. In the eighteenth century, at the invitation of the Austrian monarchy, a second wave of migrants followed, helping make the Sudetens the dominant political force in Bohemia and Moravia. The territory of these two provinces had never belonged to Germany (although they had at one time been a part of Austria-Hungary), and no one had driven the emigrants to leave their German homeland. They had migrated of their own free will. But the ancestral loyalties of this displaced people were to create difficulties for their adopted home.

When the borders of the new state of Czechoslovakia were under discussion at the Paris peace conference, the Sudeten Germans attempted to have the territory joined to Austria or Germany, but these efforts were blocked by the French delegation, which argued for keeping the Sudetenland within Czechoslovakia so that the new state would be large enough to block Germany on the east. Because the Sudetenland contained most of the industry needed to get the new state off to a good start, it also seemed economically sound to leave the borders much as they had been for centuries. Consequently, the ancient southeastern border of Germany remained unchanged except for slight alterations.

But the Sudetens resented the decisions of the conference, and refused to cooperate with the new Czechoslovak government until 1926, when they realized they could expect no help from Berlin. To further complicate the situation, they had become embittered by the depression, and they blamed the economic situation on their government. Therefore, when the Nazis came to power in Germany, they had no difficulty in revitalizing the Sudeten German party, a small Nazi organization led by Konrad Henlein. Subsidized by Berlin, the party agitated for

Sudeten autonomy, a policy that would be harmful to Czechoslovak security because the Sudetenland contained important fortifications against Germany. However, the demand for autonomy concealed Henlein's real goal, which was the eventual inclusion of Bohemia and Moravia within the German Reich. Once the area had been incorporated within Germany, then the rest of Czechoslovakia would be defenseless against Hitler's armies.

On March 28, 1938, Hitler personally instructed Henlein to make such outrageous demands of the government that it would be impossible to meet them. In return for Henlein's assistance, Hitler pledged full personal support for his new "viceroy." Speaking for Hitler, Ribbentrop emphasized to Henlein the next day that the Sudeten German party must not expect to be more than a front for the Reich, but that it must present itself as the spokesman for the campaign of the German minority to achieve complete autonomy. Whatever enticement the Czechs might offer, Henlein must not accept an invitation to join the Czechoslovak government. Henlein and the Sudeten German party must endeavor to make their subversion appear to be simply a minority seeking self-determination in the face of alleged persecution, thereby arousing the sympathies of countries already troubled by the Versailles treaty.

At the Sudeten Party Congress in Karlsbad on April 24, Henlein, following instructions, called for a series of changes in the government of the Sudetenland. He wanted the Sudetens recognized as a "legal entity," with an autonomous government staffed by Sudeten officials; and those Sudetens who lived outside the autonomous areas must be provided with legal protection. He insisted that Sudetens were to be compensated for all the financial losses suffered at the hands of the government since 1918. Finally, the Sudetens should be permitted complete freedom to profess a German ideology—nazism.

If the government were to grant these demands, the result would be a Nazi state within the boundaries of Czechoslovakia and very near the German border. But Henlein did not intend for the Karlsbad demands to be fulfilled; he meant only to harass the Czechoslovak government, to hamper its relations with Britain and France, and to build the impression that the Sudetenland had been torn from Germany by the Treaty of Versailles.

The relations of Czechoslovakia with Britain and France were the special concern of Eduard Benes, the president of Czechoslovakia. Benes had, with Thomas Masaryk, been one of the founders of the new state, and distinguished himself in international affairs as the first Czechoslovak Foreign Minister. He had negotiated a treaty of mutual assistance with France as a corollary to the Locarno Pact wherein both nations promised to come to the aid of the other in case of unprovoked attack; and he was also responsible for a treaty with Russia pledging aid to each other if one were attacked without provocation, but with the provision that France must first come to the aid of the victim. Benes thought that these treaties were sufficient to protect Czechoslovakia.

He had no difficulty in recognizing the dangers in Henlein's program: not only would it damage the Czech defenses, but it would also create a dangerous precedent, prompting other minorities to demand similar privileges and further weakening the already precarious national unity. With many autonomous groups competing for national rights, the nation might easily fall apart. To preserve Czechoslovakia as a political entity, Benes bargained and negotiated to try to restrict Sudeten demands.

However, in London and Paris, those who sought to appease Hitler regarded the efforts of Benes as dangerous to peace. To Neville Chamberlain, Czechoslovakia was a threat to the peace as long as the Sudetenland was an object of dispute. It was not simply that Chamberlain feared an invasion of Czechoslovakia by Hitler's armies, although this was one of his considerations. But under the influence of German propaganda, he also considered the Sudeten complaints of Czech discrimination to be wholly just. Chamberlain was certain that the only way to prevent German armies from overrunning Czechoslovakia was to appease the Germans. He also believed that, should there be a war over this area, any peace settlement would be forced to give the Sudetenland to Germany simply to prevent future clashes.

In order to avoid the alliances that could make peace-keeping troublesome, Chamberlain would not commit Britain to Czechoslovakia except as specified by the Covenant of the League of Nations, which called upon the members of the League to protect the territorial integrity and independence of every member of the League of Nations against aggression. On March 24, he explained to the House of Commons that these obligations would not, without careful consideration, be interpreted in any way that would endanger British interests. If, because of the Locarno Pact, France became involved in war with Germany, Chamberlain was willing only to infer that Britain could be drawn into the conflict. By avoiding a precise warning, he hoped to be able to deter any German action against France without having to resort to fighting. Any chance, however, that Chamberlain might take a firm stand against German aggression was weakened by a report on March 28 from the British Chiefs of Staff stating that Britain was unprepared for war and that war absolutely must be avoided at that time so that the nation could gain time for rearmament. In 1938, they reported, a war against Germany could mean defeat for Britain.

Whatever policy Britain should choose would greatly concern France, particularly the new government headed by Premier Edouard Daladier and Foreign Minister Georges Bonnet. Although Daladier was well aware of Hitler's drive to dominate Europe, he had no wish to support Czechoslovakia if it meant a war with Germany. As for Bonnet, he believed that a war over Czechoslovakia would be a worse disaster for France than the Franco-Prussian War had been. Bonnet preferred any sacrifice to avoid a war with Germany.

The spirits of Daladier and Bonnet were not heartened when they conferred with Chamberlain and Halifax in London on April 28 and 29. Influenced by the report of his Chiefs of Staff, Chamberlain lamented British military unpreparedness and told Daladier that he could expect only two underequipped divisions if there should be a war with Germany. Reluctantly he agreed to staff discussions on air and naval assistance. Although Daladier continually warned him against Hitler, Chamberlain could not believe Hitler wanted to destroy Czechoslovakia. Because his Chiefs of Staff had indicated that Czechoslovakia could be saved only by a full-scale war, the Prime Minister was unwilling to attempt to bluff the Fuehrer. Instead, he insisted that the Czechoslovak government must accept Henlein's demands. Unwilling to defend Czechoslovakia without Britain, Daladier and Bonnet capitulated: they would join with Chamberlain to push Prague into making concessions.

London and Paris assured the German Foreign Ministry that Prague would be instructed to seek a settlement through direct negotiations with the Sudeten Germans. Prague soon learned that it would have no support from Britain or France as long as it opposed the Sudeten demands. Negotiations must continue until a comprehensive settlement could be reached, one that would encompass all of the Sudeten demands.

However, before negotiations could begin, a new crisis erupted: on May 19, with no explanation, Henlein left the country for Austria. The government had no way of knowing how to interpret the action. Was he on his way to Hitler to receive the orders that would bring on a coup? Rumors were circulating about German troop movement and Luftwaffe reconnaissance flights near the Czech frontier. Torrents of abuse against the Czech nation poured from the Nazi presses. Late on May 20, the frightened Prague cabinet called up reservists who continued to move to their posts late into the night, expecting German bombers at any moment. When dawn came, the Czech troops were at their posts, but there had been no German attack.

As a result of the rumors and the seemingly imminent German attack, the British government announced with some reluctance that, if a conflict should occur and France should intervene, Britain could become involved. In Paris, Bonnet was terrified that the Czech mobilization might provoke Hitler into action. Once aroused, Hitler could be expected to turn on Paris, which, it was feared, "would be destroyed meter by meter through German air attacks." [6] Nevertheless, Bonnet did announce that France would stand behind its pledge to give military assistance to Czechoslovakia, but he hoped that "Germany would do nothing to put France in the position where her treaty obligations would oblige her to intervene." [7]

When German officials denied that they were preparing an invasion, they were probably telling the truth. There was an increase in military traffic, but this was apparently due to the integration of Austrian army units into the Wehrmacht combined with the usual movement of troops on regular training maneuvers. There is also the possibility that some German troops were directed eastward to test the Czech reaction. Also, the Czechs could have deliberately exaggerated the crisis to involve France and Britain more deeply in their cause.

By May 23, when Henlein returned from Germany, the crisis had died down, but its effects lingered. London and Paris exerted greater pressure on the Czechs to grant concessions to the Sudeten Germans. To Berlin, the crisis revealed the Czechoslovak determination to fight. Within Czechoslovakia, the crisis had the effect of giving the Czechoslovak army the opportunity to practice mobilization.

Actually, on April 21, Hitler had discussed his plan for the invasion of Czechoslovakia—known as *Operation Green*—with Keitel; and a preliminary directive had been begun, but it was

[6] Bullitt to Hull, May 22, 1938, *Foreign Relations of the United States, 1938*, I, pp. 512–515.
[7] Phipps to Halifax, May 22, 1938, *Documents on British Foreign Policy*, Third Series, I, p. 340.

unfinished at the time of the crisis of May 20. On May 28, to an audience consisting of Goering, Ribbentrop, Neurath, General Ludwig Beck, Keitel, Brauchitsch, and Raeder, Hitler announced: "It is my unshakeable will that Czechoslovakia shall disappear from the map." [8] The problem of living space had to be solved quickly. Should Germany attempt to acquire this needed *Lebensraum*, however, Hitler was certain that they would face opposition from Britain and France. In anticipation of a war against the nations of western Europe, Germany must first get rid of the threat to the east—Czechoslovakia. Since it was apparent that Britain and France wanted to avoid war, and since no other powers would oppose Germany, Hitler ordered his generals to complete the fortifications facing France and to complete the plans for the invasion of Czechoslovakia before Britain and France rearmed and while they were still involved with Italy over the Spanish Civil War.

On May 30, Hitler signed a directive for an invasion of Czechoslovakia to be launched no later than October 1, 1938. It was his intention to "smash Czechoslovakia by military action in the near future," [9] utilizing whatever opportunity might offer the best chance for success. He ordered immediate preparations to exploit any incident that would offer a valid excuse for war. They must use surprise and speed in wiping out the Czechoslovak forces to present western Europe with a *fait accompli*. In order to achieve this swift conquest of Czechoslovakia and to make any Anglo-French intervention pointless, all of the might of the Wehrmacht would have to be turned on Czechoslovakia, with only a screening force for the western border. When the hopelessness of the Czechoslovak cause had become apparent, Hitler expected other nations, chiefly Poland and Hungary, which had territorial claims on Czechoslovakia, to intervene. If Britain and France did intervene, *Operation Green* would have

---

[8] Wiedemann memorandum, *Documents on German Foreign Policy,* Series D, VII, p. 632.

[9] Directive for *Operation Green,* May 30, 1938, in *ibid.,* II, p. 358.

to be continued until there was nothing left of Czechoslovakia; then all of the Wehrmacht would be turned on the West.

Although Hitler still intended to exploit whatever opportunity that developed, the May 30 directive omitted all reference to freeing the "oppressed" Sudeten Germans. The omission was not accidental; Hitler had merely used the Sudetens to conceal his goals.

Throughout the spring and early summer of 1938, while Germany proceeded with preparations for war, the Czechoslovak government had great difficulty with the Sudeten negotiations. Whatever Prague proposed, the Sudetens always found an excuse to reject. From Berlin, the Nazi press hurled threats at the people of Czechoslovakia; and from London and Paris came pleas for immediate concessions to all the Sudeten demands—although both governments knew very well that German military preparations were underway and that a German attack on Czechoslovakia was planned for the autumn.

To hasten a settlement before there could be a war, Chamberlain and Halifax adopted a new method: they dispatched a mediator to Czechoslovakia to bring both parties to agreement. Walter Runciman, a millionaire shipbuilder, was chosen to undertake this task. However, he lacked one important qualification: he had no experience in European minority problems. Chamberlain publicly announced that Runciman would be acting only in a personal capacity; but the truth was that he was an official agent of the British government, and he had been instructed to force Benes to accept a solution that would be pleasing to the Sudeten Germans and to Hitler.

Chamberlain and Halifax had blackmailed Benes into accepting Runciman as a mediator, threatening that, if he should refuse, they would leak the fact to the newspapers. Then the Czechoslovak government would stand condemned for turning down peaceful mediation.

Runciman reached Prague early in August, and immediately he was inundated by a mountain of Sudeten memoranda, articles, and documents that were intended to convince him that the problem could not be solved under the existing circumstances. Runciman aggravated matters by spending his weekends in the homes of wealthy Sudetens, who filled his ears with stories of their suffering countrymen. He came to believe these tales and endeavored to force Benes into granting all of the Sudeten demands. At last Benes realized that, if he wanted to hold the sympathy of Britain and France, he had no alternative but to give in.

Early in September, the Czechoslovak cabinet offered the Sudeten leaders most of the Karlsbad demands. Suddenly the Sudetens were faced with the awful prospect of accepting the cabinet's proposals or risking exposure of their plot. However, they were rescued from this dilemma by a riot in a Czech town. On September 7, when a group of Sudeten deputies visited fellow party members who had been imprisoned for gun-running, a demonstration by the Sudeten Germans erupted, which soon attracted curious Czechs. In the process of breaking up the demonstration, the police managed to rough up some of the deputies, giving the Sudetens the excuse of police brutality to halt the negotiations. The government moved quickly to make amends by firing the policemen involved, and the negotiations were scheduled to resume on September 13.

However, on September 12, in a speech broadcast to the world, Hitler denounced the Czechoslovak government for its treatment of the Sudeten minority:

The misery of the Sudeten Germans is indescribable. It is sought to annihilate them. As human beings they are oppressed and scandalously treated in an intolerable fashion. When three and a half million members of a people which numbers nearly eighty million may not sing a song they like simply because it does not please the Czechs, or when they are beaten until the blood flows solely because they wear stockings the sight of which offends the Czechs, or when they are terrorized and ill-treated because they use a form of greeting which the Czechs dislike, . . . when they are hunted and harried like helpless wild fowl for every expression of national sentiment—this may perhaps cause the worthy representatives of our democracies no concern: they may possibly welcome it since in this case only some three and a half million Germans are in question; but I can only say to the representatives of these democracies that this does concern us, and that if these tortured creatures can of themselves find no justice and no help they will get both from us. The depriving of these people of their rights must come to an end.[10]

Before his tirade ended, the riots had exploded into civil war in the Sudetenland, forcing Prague to dispatch troops. Again, the Sudeten leaders broke off negotiations. Henlein fled across the frontier; and, from the safety of Germany, he issued a proclamation calling for the "return" of the Sudetenland to the German Reich. At last, they had been able to give the world the impression that Germany had a right to the Sudetenland, and Hitler would be able to press for the direct inclusion of the territory within the German nation.

When the news of the fighting in the Sudetenland reached Paris, Daladier begged Chamberlain to do whatever he could to prevent war. By doing this, he was, in effect, delivering French foreign policy into the hands of the British Prime Minister. For some time Chamberlain had been considering a personal meeting with Hitler; and now, without consulting either the British, French, or Czechoslovak cabinets, he requested an invitation from Hitler to visit Germany and confer with him. Astonished but delighted by the request, Hitler extended the invitation; and, in search of peace, the British politician embarked on his first airplane ride.

Hitler and Chamberlain met on September 15 at Berchtesgaden. After a pleasant tea, they held their conference—in the same room where Schuschnigg and Hitler had met in February. Hitler threatened war if the Sudetenland were not given to the Reich. If Hitler was so determined on war, Chamberlain indicated that he might as well return to London. Realizing that he

[10] *Documents on International Affairs 1938* (London, 1943), II, p. 193.

had gone too far, Hitler proposed that the Sudetenland could be ceded to Germany on the basis of self-determination, in line with Chamberlain's thinking. Mollified, Chamberlain promised to do what he could to give Hitler what he wanted.

However, when Chamberlain returned to London, he encountered opposition. Two cabinet meetings on September 17 produced no agreement, with some members opposed to any commitments whatever beyond the Rhine. Duff Cooper, First Lord of the Admiralty, voiced fears that Hitler might achieve the position of dominating the entire continent of Europe. And some cabinet members rejected the cession because other minorities in Czechoslovakia might demand the same procedure for themselves.

On September 18 and 19, Daladier and Bonnet came to London for a conference with Chamberlain and Halifax. When confronted with the Hitler–Chamberlain solution, Daladier rejected the use of self-determination through a plebiscite lest it open up all of Central Europe to Hitler. But Daladier's generals had warned him before he left Paris that Germany possessed the strength to crush Czechoslovakia in only a few days. With this in mind, he accepted Chamberlain's proposal. To satisfy the French, Chamberlain promised to guarantee the new Czechoslovakia. Here was a genuine revolution in British foreign policy: Chamberlain had promised that Britain would guarantee a frontier deep in Central Europe, far from the English Channel. Nothing comparable had occurred since the agreement with Frederick the Great in 1756 to guarantee Prussia.

Benes and his cabinet rejected the Anglo-French proposal and insisted upon arbitration of the matter. But London and Paris changed their proposal to an ultimatum: unless Czechoslovakia accepted the proposal, Chamberlain would cease his efforts to avert war and France would refuse aid to Czechoslovakia if war broke out. On September 21, the Czechoslovak cabinet capitulated; and, on September 22, Chamberlain met

Hitler again, this time at Godesberg. Believing that he had saved Europe from war, the Prime Minister reported to Hitler as a chairman of the board would address an annual stockholders meeting. He was certainly not prepared for the response he was to receive from Hitler. The report was unacceptable to the Fuehrer. The injustices suffered by all the minorities in Czechoslovakia had to be redressed. There were Polish and Hungarian demands that had already arisen and must be settled if peace were to be established in Central Europe. The frontier between Germany and Czechoslovakia must be drawn immediately and must be based on language. Czechoslovak soldiers must be withdrawn from the new German territory at once, and a German occupation force must be allowed into the ceded area. Chamberlain wanted—and thought he had effected—a more leisurely take-over. The Fuehrer and the Prime Minister exchanged angry words, and the meeting ended in deadlock.

The next day Hitler sent Chamberlain a memorandum spelling out his demands. The evacuation of the Sudetenland would commence on September 26 and be over by the 28th. The entire area must be handed over to the Germans without damage to property or installations; nothing could be evacuated except people. A map attached to the memorandum indicated the areas that the German troops would occupy; in effect, Germany would be occupying sufficient area to cripple Czechoslovak defenses.

Meeting again with Hitler in the evening of September 23, Chamberlain again objected to Hitler's demand for immediate occupation, but the Fuehrer insisted on a speedy solution to a problem that had been left unsolved for twenty years. Chamberlain complained about Hitler's memorandum sounding so much like an ultimatum. And the occupation of areas that were not ethnically German disturbed him. Hitler spurned Chamberlain's complaints and made only one concession: the Czech evacuation did not have to begin until October 1—the final date he had considered for *Operation Green*.

On September 24, before the conference ended, the Czechs had mobilized their armed forces and refused the Godesberg demands. At first, the French cabinet reluctantly agreed to stand by their ally; but, in a conference with Chamberlain, Halifax, Simon, and Hoare in London on September 25 and 26, Daladier and Bonnet were unable to come up with joint war plans. Instead, the Englishmen occupied the meeting with interrogating the Frenchmen about their plans and preparations and trying to pressure them to abandon Czechoslovakia to Hitler. Only after he was convinced that Daladier was determined to support Czechoslovakia did Chamberlain promise British aid to France, but he made no pledge of direct help to Czechoslovakia. If France should decide not to fight, then Britain had no obligation.

On September 26, Chamberlain dispatched Sir Horace Wilson, his special advisor, to Hitler to convey the results of the Anglo-French meeting. Wilson was unable, in his two violent interviews with Hitler, to receive any significant response from the Fuehrer. Instead of responding, Hitler raved incoherently about Britain and France attacking Germany because the Czechs had precipitated a war by rejecting his demands. In a speech in the Sportpalast on September 26, Hitler implied that war was near unless the Sudetens were permitted to rejoin Germany; but in his official answer to Chamberlain, which arrived in London by letter on September 27, he promised to guarantee the integrity of the remainder of Czechoslovakia as well as to guarantee favorable treatment for Czechs remaining in the German-occupied territory. However, he continued to insist upon immediate occupation to halt the Czech delaying tactics. The final frontiers could always be straightened out later by plebiscite and negotiation.

The conciliatory tone of the letter implied that Hitler had changed, but he had written it simply for publication, as was evidenced by his quick permission to London to publish the letter. It is probable that the letter was drafted to avoid the kind of propaganda defeat Germany had received in 1914, when the ultimatums to Russia, France, and Belgium, followed by declarations of war, had given Germany the onus of aggressor. Nevertheless, Europe braced itself for what was expected to come. In London and Paris, art collections were stowed away while trenches were dug in parks, gas masks were distributed to the public, anti-aircraft batteries were set up, and children were evacuated to the country. Prague ordered a blackout. And, in Berlin, Hitler ordered the first assault units to attack at 6:15 AM on September 30.

But the concern was not limited merely to France, Britain, and Czechoslovakia. In the United States, Franklin D. Roosevelt twice asked that negotiations resume, pointing out that the negotiators had already reached the most difficult hurdle of agreement in principle. Nor were the demands being made entirely by Germany. Polish Foreign Minister Jozef Beck demanded that Czechoslovakia immediately cede Teschen to Poland, and Hungary grew bold enough to request equal treatment for the Magyars living within Czechoslovakia. Although the Soviet Union would not become involved in a German–Czechoslovak conflict unless France should aid Czechoslovakia first, Soviet Commissar for Foreign Affairs Maxim Litvinov managed a threat to denounce the Soviet non-aggression pact with Poland if Polish troops should cross the Czechoslovak frontier. However, the Poles were not impressed.

But Chamberlain continued to labor for peace. Late on September 27, he appealed to Hitler with a new plan, providing for occupation of the Sudetenland according to a timetable. That night, he spoke to the nation in a radio broadcast:

How horrible, fantastic, incredible it is that we should be digging trenches and trying on gas masks here because of a quarrel in a faraway country between people of whom we know nothing. It seems still more impossible that a quarrel which has already been settled in principle should be the subject of war. . . . However much we may sympathize with a small nation confronted by a big, powerful neighbor, we cannot in all circumstances undertake to involve the whole British Empire in a war simply on her account. If we have to fight, it must be on larger issues than that.[11]

He followed this with another message to Hitler dispatched on the morning of September 28, announcing that he was prepared to come to Berlin to negotiate with Czechoslovak, Italian, and French representatives, promising that Britain and France would force Czechoslovakia to abide by the decisions of the conference. To reinforce this suggestion, Chamberlain had the British ambassador in Rome appeal to Mussolini to use his influence with Hitler. Frightened by the possibility of a war for which Italy was unprepared, Mussolini begged Hitler to accept the conference. The French ambassador in Berlin reinforced the new move by presenting a plan drafted by Bonnet calling for German troops to occupy important sections of the Sudetenland no later than October 1; France also promised to compel Czechoslovakia to fall into line.

With three capitals courting Hitler and promising so much to satisfy his demands, war would have been hard to justify. By September 28, no nation—not even Czechoslovakia—continued to dispute Hitler's claims to the Sudetenland; the only disagreement was over the way the territory was to change hands. Britain and France had now offered him a blank check; the Soviet Union had indicated they would not intervene; and Poland, eager to get in on the spoils, offered no opposition. Under these conditions, Hitler could not insist on war, so he accepted the proposal for a conference provided Mussolini could come. The Duce accepted joyfully. In the afternoon of September 28, invitations from Berlin for a summit conference to be held at Munich were dispatched to Daladier and Chamberlain—but no invitation was sent to Prague.

[11] Neville Chamberlain, *In Search of Peace* (New York, 1939), pp. 174–175.

Chamberlain received the message about the conference while he was detailing the story of the summer's negotiations to the House of Commons. He announced to a quiet, intent House of Commons: "I have now been informed by Herr Hitler that he invites me to meet him at Munich tomorrow morning. He has also invited Signor Mussolini and M. Daladier. Signor Mussolini has accepted and I have no doubt M. Daladier will also accept. I need not say what my answer will be." [12] The members broke into cheers, with only a handful keeping silent.

Besides the obvious reason for Hitler's acceptance of the conference, there were several pressures on him that were not so apparent. Some of his generals had expressed great concern over weaknesses in the western defenses, and Army Chief of Staff General Ludwig Beck had resigned in protest against Hitler's provoking a European war when he believed that Germany was unprepared. There is also the possibility that Chamberlain's promise to support France may have shaken Hitler's confidence that Britain was going to avoid war at all costs.

A few conspirators had communicated with London, begging Chamberlain to stand firm, call Hitler's bluff, and if necessary begin the war. Then the German generals would overthrow Hitler. Chamberlain rejected this plea because the past conduct of the German officer corps did not warrant trusting them in 1938. Had Chamberlain called Hitler's bluff and war broken out, the plot would surely have failed. Obscure German politicians and some conservative officers could never have aroused soldiers already converted to nazism to overthrow their popular Fuehrer in the midst of a war. The stench of treason would have been too strong.

Was Hitler bluffing? Did he accept the Munich Conference because Chamberlain called his bluff? Most of his contemporaries believed he was determined on war, not bluffing. Actually, it would be impossible to ascertain, because his bluff was never

[12] *Parliamentary Debates, House of Commons,* Fifth Series, vol. 339, cols. 26–28.

called. Too many wanted to avoid doing that, and when it was called finally in September 1939, war did come.

Certainly, Hitler had accepted the conference knowing that he would be able to dominate the meetings, overawe Daladier and Chamberlain, and win a personal victory. After all, his claims had been guaranteed in advance; war had become unnecessary unless he sought it himself.

THE MUNICH CONFERENCE

About noon on September 29, the conference opened at Munich in the Fuehrerhaus. All of the principals at the meeting agreed with Hitler's insistence on speed; but, without a chairman and an agenda, the discussion wandered from topic to topic. Finally, Mussolini presented a memorandum that had been drafted in the German Foreign Ministry and had been handed to him before the conference opened. Because Chamberlain and Daladier had nothing to offer, this memorandum became the basis for discussion. The proceedings became extremely legalistic, with Chamberlain efficiently inquiring about such technical details as the relocation of cattle. With this, Hitler soon became unhappy because it limited his opportunities for frightening Daladier and Chamberlain. But Mussolini bustled about, enjoying the conference, thinking that he had been responsible for averting war.

Because no one kept out the uninvited, the conference room came to resemble a railroad station during a holiday weekend. At no time during the conference did Chamberlain and Daladier confer privately, although they did have the opportunity during a recess; and, late in the evening, the final drafts of the agreement were prepared. Early in the morning of September 30, the agreement was signed by the four heads of government.

The contents of the Munich Agreement called for the evacuation of Czechoslovak forces from an area that was designated on an attached map, beginning on October 1 and reaching completion by October 10. At the same time, in four stages, German troops would occupy the area. Conditions for the evacuation and occupation would be decided by an international commission with representatives from the four signatory powers plus Czechoslovakia. This commission would not only determine any additional areas to be occupied but also administer plebiscites and draw the final frontier. The British and French governments promised to guarantee the new frontiers against unprovoked aggression, but Italy and Germany would guarantee the new frontiers only after Hungarian and Polish claims had been satisfied. Czech compliance with the terms was mandatory.

Under the terms of the Munich Agreement, an independent nation lost vital territory containing important fortifications without a battle being fought. It was comparable only to the partition of Poland in the eighteenth century. At the Paris Peace Conference and after a long war, Germany had been permitted to submit objections to the terms of the Versailles treaty in writing; but, in 1938, even this was denied Czechoslovakia. The Czech representatives who came to Munich were simply summoned before Chamberlain and Daladier and informed that Czechoslovakia was considered to have already accepted the Munich Agreement and that there would be no appeal from this decision.

In the early morning hours of September 30, at his own request, Chamberlain met privately with Hitler without informing Daladier. The Prime Minister produced a statement on Anglo-German relations, carefully typed in duplicate, which he asked Hitler to sign. According to the statement, Hitler and Chamberlain regarded the Munich Agreement and the Anglo-German Naval Agreement as "symbolic of the desire of our two peoples never to go to war with one another again." In the future, "consultations" would be used to handle questions concerning Britain and Germany. They resolved to "continue our efforts to remove possible sources of difference and thus to contribute to assure the peace of Europe." [13] Hitler, tired and sleepy, signed the agreement without fully realizing what the elderly Englishman had done.

Chamberlain had managed to obtain Hitler's written promise to meet with him before making further territorial claims. It had been agreed that, henceforth, Anglo-German diplomacy would be conducted face-to-face by these two men. Together they would insure the peace of Europe. The businesslike Prime Minister was confident: he expected Hitler to consult him as would any businessman who had signed a contract. But, although he had managed to obtain this small diplomatic victory, he had not secured "peace in our time," for Hitler did not view the sanctity of contracts in quite the same way as Chamberlain. He considered the statement as simply another indication that Britain would not block his plans in eastern Europe.

Shortly after noon on September 30, the Czechoslovak government formally accepted the agreement. The betrayed Czechoslovak people wept openly in the streets of Prague, while their soldiers began withdrawing from positions they had lost without a battle. Some of the generals did want to fight, but Benes ordered the withdrawal because the only alternative was a war fought alone against Germany, Poland, and possibly Hungary, and the Czechoslovak government would have been condemned for starting the war. A week after the Munich Conference, Benes resigned under German pressure and soon left Czechoslovakia.

Chamberlain and Daladier returned to their capitals to be lauded for their labors in behalf of peace. They were showered with gifts, and honors—such as streets being named for them— were heaped upon them. It was a time of rejoicing for the appeasers. However, Daladier was able to see the damage that had been done to European security, although he kept silent for political reasons. France had suffered a grievous defeat, and he

[13] The Anglo-German Declaration, September 30, 1938, *Documents on German Foreign Policy,* Series D, II, p. 1017.

realized that its position as a major European power was gone.

Although Chamberlain eventually was able to comprehend something of the enormity of the diplomatic defeat suffered at Munich, he was never really able to understand Hitler or the strategic importance of Czechoslovakia. He saw the crisis as "a quarrel in a faraway country between people of whom we know nothing." [14] His critics had wanted Chamberlain to call Hitler's bluff, but that was not Chamberlain's way of doing things. Perhaps more important, he knew that Britain was unprepared, both psychologically and militarily, for war against Germany; and he knew that, if he attempted to bluff Hitler, there would certainly have been a war. Chamberlain could not see the Sudetenland as a valid reason for the slaughter of millions, especially since the Sudetens wanted to be German anyway. Furthermore, he had confidence that, once this question was settled, Hitler would have no more territorial demands. Chamberlain's decision was also influenced by the opinions of the governments of the dominions, which were united in their opposition to war. The high commissioners of Australia, New Zealand, Canada, and South Africa pressured Chamberlain to accept Hitler's Godesberg demands.

Britain did gain some benefits from the September crisis, however. The British military services were able to test their defenses and their mobilization plans; and, in the year's delay gained by the Munich Agreement, British military power increased proportionately more than Germany's. But the French failed to make efficient use of the time. There was a slight increase in aircraft production, which the government exaggerated; but the nation continued to suffer from internal problems, with generally poor productivity throughout the armament industries and with the trade unions directly opposing the acceleration of armaments production.

The Soviet Union (particularly Joseph Stalin) benefited

[14] Chamberlain, *op. cit.*, p. 174.

greatly from the Munich Conference, for the Soviet government was able to pose as a firm opponent of nazism and, at the same time, evade its obligations to Czechoslovakia. Nevertheless, western powers have been severely criticized by some for their failure to turn to Stalin for help. These critics have interpreted Maxim Litvinov's pious declarations in behalf of collective security to mean that Soviet aid against Hitler would be readily available if requested. However, as Stalin's spokesman, Litvinov was careful not to commit his master to any action that might require the use of military force, for Stalin had never been as eager to aid Czechoslovakia against Nazi Germany as some had imagined. The pacts that Litvinov had negotiated with Czechoslovakia and France were intended only to protect Russia from possible German attacks; they were not intended as a definite Russian commitment to either France or Czechoslovakia. In diplomatic conferences, spokesmen for the Soviet Union avoided explaining precisely how their country might aid Czechoslovakia, and they always tacked qualifying conditions onto what promises they did make.

At the time of the crisis in September 1938, Russia made no military preparations in case Czechoslovakia required help, because Stalin had no intention of sending aid. Litvinov disappeared from public view late in September, reappearing on October 1—after the crisis was over—to denounce Britain and France. If they had stood firm, he claimed, "they would, with Russian help, have made Hitler climb down."[15] But he had offered no help when it could have been used. In June, Litvinov had criticized the western powers and indicated that the Soviet Union would not be responsible for future developments, and in August, he had notified Berlin that the Soviet Union considered the Sudeten question an internal affair of Czechoslovakia and not a matter that would concern Moscow.

In looking back on the situation, it was certainly true that

15 Phipps to Halifax, October 1, 1938, *Documents on British Foreign Policy,* Third Series, III, p. 67.

neither Britain nor France was prepared for war. In Britain, only the Royal Navy had any degree of combat readiness, and the R.A.F. was faced with a shortage of new planes, weapons, and pilots. Anti-aircraft guns and searchlights were in short supply. And, most important of all, the radar chain that was to save Britain in 1940 had not yet been completed in 1938. Although France possessed a larger army than Germany, the French generals planned in case of war to hold their troops within the Maginot Line while Polish and German armies finished off Czechoslovakia. The French General Staff had made no plans for joint action with either Czechoslovakia or Britain.

But it is also true that the German military, although ready for a *Blitzkrieg* war against Czechoslovakia, was unprepared for a full-scale world war in 1938. Along the Czechoslovak borders, there were forty divisions, but only five divisions were available to protect Germany from an invasion by France. There were inadequate forces to withstand any attack through East Prussia. The Luftwaffe was strong enough to attack Czechoslovakia but it could put up only a weak defense in the west.

Finally, the fact that there was peace instead of war as a result of the Munich Agreement pleased those people in Europe who believed that the Sudeten cause was just and that a war in behalf of Czechoslovakia was immoral. They were convinced that peace was worth the price of ceding the Sudetenland to Germany. In their longing to avoid war, it appeared moral to them to sacrifice the Czechoslovak people to appease Hitler and give Europe peace.

THE END OF CZECHOSLOVAKIA

Although the appeasers celebrated the Munich Agreement, the cession of the Sudetenland was only a temporary measure as far as Hitler was concerned. He was simply waiting for his next opportunity to reach out for *Lebensraum*. Having gained the advantage in Czechoslovakia, he was not going to be satisfied with just the Sudetenland. At every opportunity, German troops acting under Hitler's orders pushed past the limits of the occupation zone specified by the Munich Agreement. Once they had occupied Czechoslovak territory, it became German.

Except for a few vain efforts from the Czech delegate, the five-power international commission—consisting of Germany, Italy, France, Britain, and Czechoslovakia—that had been established to supervise the implementation of the Munich Agreement offered no protest. German diplomats and generals dominated the meetings. In determining the final frontier, the international commission, at Ribbentrop's insistence, used a 1910 census that was more favorable to Germany than a later one would have been. And the settlement was complicated by the incursions of German troops past the limits of the occupation zone. Once they had violated the temporary frontier, Hitler forbade their withdrawal. Because it was unthinkable that German troops would give up territory they had occupied, the frontier was finally decided not by the international commission but by a German ultimatum giving Czechoslovakia a forty-eight-hour time limit to accept the frontier as determined by the German troops. After the Czechs capitulated, the international commission solemnly ratified the frontier.

But the Czech-Sudeten minority problem had not been settled. Rather, it had been further complicated, because there were over 478,000 Sudetens remaining within Czechoslovakia. Hitler had not wanted plebiscites to determine the future of these Sudetens: by leaving them in Czechoslovakia, he would have an additional minority problem to exploit if he needed it. In addition to this, however, there were over 670,000 Czechs caught within the new German frontiers. By mutual consent of Germany and Czechoslovakia, the Munich Agreement provisions for plebiscites were ignored, since the results of plebiscites could have altered the frontiers drastically to the detriment of either or both countries, thus disrupting the plans of Hitler's generals and creating new minority problems for the Czechoslovak government.

As it was, the concessions to Germany had already set off

further boundary disputes. Poland and Hungary used their national minorities within Czechoslovakia to obtain territory for themselves. Poland's pretension to the status of a great power had been ignored by the planners of the Munich Conference. But the cession of the Sudetenland had opened the way for Beck to obtain the status he sought by dispatching an ultimatum to Prague on September 30 demanding the cession of Teschen, the area taken from Poland in 1920. Under pressure from London and Paris, the Czechs again complied. Because Poland could not have acquired Teschen without Hitler, Poland became indebted to him. And Hitler would expect repayment of the debt.

The breakup of Czechoslovakia continued with Hungarian claims for the territory that was occupied by Magyars. No loss of territory had angered the Hungarians more than the land that had been taken from them in 1919 to extend the southern frontier of Slovakia. Because the Hungarians had not pushed their claims hard enough to satisfy him, Hitler did not press their cause at the Munich Conference, forcing Hungary to resort to its own negotiations with Czechoslovakia. After these negotiations collapsed in October, both countries appealed to the Munich powers to settle the dispute. Britain and France chose to relinquish all responsibility in the matter to Germany and Italy, thereby magnifying the prestige of the Fascist powers. Ribbentrop and Ciano, acting for their governments on November 2, decided in favor of Hungary, giving the Magyar state a territory with a population of over one million people.

These changes in the map of Central Europe were all proof of increasing German dominance. London accepted this as a fact of life, as inescapable. Halifax regarded it as "inevitable for obvious geographical and economic reasons." In his view, "German expansion in Central Europe . . . [was] a normal and natural thing." [16]

Eager to take advantage of the friendly atmosphere of the

[16] Halifax to Phipps, November 1, 1938, *Documents on British Foreign Policy*, Third Series, III, p. 252.

Munich Conference, Chamberlain began to work out an economic approach to appeasement. He hoped that he could pacify Germany by granting economic advantages, thereby making Germany's territorial grabs unnecessary. Britain offered Germany large credits and proposed new agreements on Anglo-German trade that would be extremely beneficial to Germany. In negotiations, the Germans were astounded at the eagerness of British trade delegations to reach an agreement. However, negotiations achieved very little. Chamberlain had adopted his conciliatory attitude, imagining that once economic relations favored Germany confidence in Europe would be restored and peace would be strengthened through new opportunities for trade and commerce. But Hitler, who did not think exclusively in economic terms, regarded the British offers as further signs that there would be no opposition to further aggression.

When Bonnet sought a Franco-German declaration similar to the one Chamberlain had signed with Hitler on September 30, Chamberlain could not raise any objection. The suggestion was welcome in Berlin, for Hitler wanted a French promise to keep hands off his intrigues in eastern Europe. Consequently Hitler sent his personal plane to bring the French ambassador, André Francois-Poncet, to Berchtesgaden for a conference. To prove that he was a Francophile, Hitler denounced the British for causing the recent trouble over Czechoslovakia, and he appeared eager to reconcile himself with France. After this friendly meeting, the subject was pursued by the foreign ministries. By early November, the German Foreign Ministry had prepared a draft declaration for Bonnet's consideration. Despite the French Foreign Minister's desire to have an early signing of the declarations, negotiations continued into December.

The Franco-German declaration which had been drafted in Berlin, was finally signed on December 6. Ribbentrop represented Germany, and Bonnet represented France. The terms seemed innocent. Both countries acknowledged that no territorial question was outstanding, and both recognized their frontiers as final. Should there be troublesome international matters, both promised to confer. However, the talks that accompanied the signing revealed the meaning of the declaration. Ribbentrop asserted that Czechoslovakia lay within Germany's sphere of influence, and any French agreement to guarantee the integrity of the new Czechoslovakia would be looked upon as an attempt to wreck the Franco-German declaration. Friendship between France and Germany, according to Ribbentrop, was entirely dependent upon French acknowledgment of German hegemony in eastern Europe. During the conference, Bonnet had never challenged Ribbentrop's declaration; and, by his silence, he had inferred consent to it.

The Franco-German declaration, like Chamberlain's drive for economic appeasement of Germany, only encouraged Hitler in his campaign to smash Czechoslovakia, a campaign that had been halted momentarily by the Munich Conference. Shortly after the signing of the Munich Agreement, Hitler had inquired about the forces Germany would need to destroy Czechoslovak resistance. How much time would be required to move in additional troops? How much warning would the troops need to go into action? On October 21, 1938, after he had collected the answers to these questions, Hitler issued a directive for the Wehrmacht to prepare for the "liquidation" of Czechoslovakia whenever a favorable opportunity should develop. To avoid having to mobilize additional troops, thereby arousing foreign opinion, he ordered a high degree of combat readiness for the standing army. He issued a supplement to the directive in December, explaining that the liquidation must appear to be a pacification measure and not a military operation.

Throughout the winter of 1938–1939, Hitler continued his pressure on Czechoslovakia, complaining that the Czechoslovak army was too large and should be reduced, that the Prague government did not persecute the Jews as they should, and that too much of the Benes mentality remained in the nation.

For the Czechoslovak people in their winter of misery, one

hope remained—the guarantee by the Munich powers of the Czechoslovak frontiers against unprovoked aggression. Despite the attempts of Britain and France, however, this guarantee was destined never to be implemented. In order to make it palatable to Hitler, Chamberlain pressured Daladier and Bonnet to accept his interpretation of the guarantee, which was that it must have the backing of at least three of the four powers, so that Britain and France would not have to go to war against Germany and Italy over Czechoslovakia. With France in their pockets, Chamberlain and Halifax took a trip to Rome in January 1939 to try to convert Mussolini to their viewpoint, but the Duce found excuses to avoid joining in the guarantee. When the British and French governments brought up the subject in Berlin, the Fuehrer claimed that an implementation of the guarantee would serve only to foment Czechoslovak hostility towards Germany. Hitler insisted on waiting until some of the internal problems of Czechoslovakia had been settled and relations with its neighbors had improved. Hitler's categorical reply on March 3, 1939 was reason enough for Chamberlain and Daladier to cease their efforts at implementation.

Hitler avoided this guarantee because he did not want to tie himself down with yet another agreement. He was waiting for his chance to devour the remainder of Czechoslovakia, and he knew the greater the insurance of peace there, the less chance he would have to act.

Hitler found the key to the final destruction of Czechoslovakia in the Slovak minority. The Slovaks had been granted autonomy on October 6, 1938, and their premier was Monsignor Joseph Tiso, who practiced a Slovak brand of fascism. Berlin encouraged Tiso to push for complete separation. Hitler even hinted that, if the Slovaks asked him to protect their independence, he would gladly comply. With this encouragement, the Slovaks demanded that Prague permit them their own army and give them greater financial aid. The Prague government finally began to realize that, unless the Tiso government was curbed,

Czechoslovakia would degenerate into a confederation and might eventually be dissolved entirely. Prague decided to be firm, thereby providing Hitler with the opportunity he had been seeking.

On March 10, 1939, Prague dismissed the Tiso government, proclaimed martial law in Slovakia, and appointed Karol Sidor to succeed Tiso. Unable to persuade Sidor to proclaim independence, the Nazis called on Hitler for help. Berlin decided that it was necessary to continue to recognize Tiso as the legal premier. Ordering Tiso to Berlin, Hitler launched into one of his harangues. If the Slovaks wanted independence, he was willing to help and protect them, but should the Slovaks reject him, Hitler would leave them to the mercy of Hungary. Provided with a "declaration of independence" drafted by Ribbentrop and grateful for Hitler's benevolence, Tiso returned to Slovakia. He delivered the declaration of independence to the Slovak cabinet and diet and informed them of Hitler's wishes. Sidor was obliged to resign. After the cabinet and the diet unanimously approved the "independence" requested by Berlin, Hitler had his excuse to march into Czechoslovakia: he was protecting the right of self-determination.

To speed the fall of Czechoslovakia, Ribbentrop sent the Hungarian minister home to Budapest to inform his government that the time had come for them to occupy Ruthenia, the extreme eastern section of Czechoslovakia. The Hungarian government was excited at the prospect, but preferred that Germany move first. When they received news of the Slovak proclamation, Budapest dispatched an ultimatum to Prague requiring the evacuation of Ruthenia within twenty-four hours. Budapest also demanded the arming of Magyar inhabitants. Prague accepted the ultimatum but would not arm the Magyars, so Budapest found the reply unsuitable. At dawn on March 15, Hungarian troops crossed into Ruthenia. All that was left of Czechoslovakia now was a part of Bohemia and Moravia, home of the Czechs.

By March 11, an ultimatum to Prague had been drafted in

Berlin, but the Czech government was not, as yet, aware of Hitler's precise intentions. On instructions from Berlin, the German minister in Prague had been unavailable to Czech officials; and since March 13, the Czech minister in Berlin had been denied information about German intentions. In desperation, Emil Hacha, the president of Czechoslovakia, requested an audience with Hitler. Already German troops had seized towns across the Czech frontier, but Hitler received the aged president early in the morning of March 15.

Hitler put on the performance that had been denied him at Munich. He berated Hacha for the Czech hostility toward Germany and grieved over the iniquities of the ungrateful Czechs who persisted in the policies of Benes. Finally he told Hacha that German troops had been ordered to begin occupying Bohemia and Moravia at 6:00 AM. Hitler offered Hacha a choice: the Czechs could resist and be annihilated or they could accept their fate without resistance and be permitted a limited degree of national freedom. As usual with these meetings, all the necessary documents had been carefully prepared in advance. Hitler demanded that Hacha and Frantisek Chvalkovsky, the Czech Foreign Minister, sign the document and then left Goering and Ribbentrop to finish the job. Goering and Ribbentrop subjected the Czechs to shouts, curses, and insults. Twice Hacha fainted; and, at last exhausted by the ordeal, he surrendered and agreed to sign the documents. After telephone connections were established with Prague, he directed the Czech premier, Rudolf Beran, not to resist the occupying forces. Hacha and Chvalkovsky had been browbeaten into turning the Czech people over to Hitler and surrendering all of the Czech armed forces. The documents they had signed were merely for appearance, a formality undergone to show the world that Germany had not attacked Czechoslovakia. According to the published communiqué, Hacha and Chvalkovsky had taken the step only after a frank consultation with Hitler.

By this charade, Hitler had presented France and Britain

with a *fait accompli*, preventing a repetition of the Munich Conference in which Chamberlain might have become too zealous about Czechoslovak interests.

At dawn on March 15, the weather was so poor that the planes of the Luftwaffe were unable to take off; but, by 9:00 AM, German soldiers had entered Prague. The same day, German troops occupied the newly "independent" Slovakia; and by evening, Hitler was in the president's palace in Prague, where he issued a proclamation formally ending Czechoslovak independence.

In the face of Hitler's *fait accompli*, Britain and France could only protest for the record book. Neither country was willing to go to war even though Hitler's action had, in effect, torn up the Munich Agreement. Both countries, by appeasing Hitler and presenting the territory to him as a sphere of influence, had led Hitler to believe that they had written off Czechoslovakia entirely. But this had not been their intent. The appeasers had hoped that Hitler was a reasonable man and that reasonable men would seek conciliation to avoid a war as disastrous as the last. To do their share of being conciliatory, the appeasers had stretched the concept of self-determination as far as it would stretch, and they had laboriously constructed a defense for Hitler's aggression. Now, by his take-over of Czechoslovakia, he had destroyed their edifice. In the words of Bonnet, "The peace and appeasement policy of the 'men of Munich' had suffered a lamentable disaster. And now in every country warmongers who would lead Europe toward catastrophe were bound to gain the upper hand." [17]

Hitler had promised Chamberlain that he only wanted the return of Germans to the Fatherland, but the occupation of Czechoslovakia shattered that pretense. With that promise broken and with the policy of appeasement shattered, Chamberlain was faced with a political crisis. He still wanted to practice

[17] Welczek to the German Foreign Ministry, *Documents on German Foreign Policy*, Series D, IV, p. 283.

appeasement if Hitler would only let him; if Hitler would not permit appeasement, then he must begin to build some other policy, preferably continuing to avoid war.

After Halifax prevailed upon him to speak out against Hitler's action, Chamberlain voiced his first public warning on March 17. Was Hitler's action in Czechoslovakia "a step in the direction of an attempt to dominate the world by force?" If Hitler intended such a challenge, he must not imagine that "because it believes war to be a senseless and evil thing, this nation has so lost its fibre that it will not take part to the utmost of its power resisting such a challenge if it were ever made." [18] Chamberlain was still optimistic, hoping that a way could be found to avoid war.

[18] Chamberlain, *op. cit.*, pp. 274–275.

5 / War'
1939

DANZIG

The German occupation of Czechoslovakia meant that Poland was surrounded by Germany on three frontiers; and, with vital areas open to attack, Polish security was endangered. Any help from the West would have to come by sea; but, in a war involving Germany, the Baltic would literally become a German lake. In these circumstances, safety for Poland would seem to lie in seeking external protection against Germany. However, the man who was to guide Polish foreign policy through this period chose to follow other policies.

Jozef Beck, the Polish Foreign Minister, had for too long been cool to the German threat although he was not inexperienced in foreign affairs. He had been Pilsudski's *chef de cabinet,* then under-secretary in the Foreign Ministry, before finally becoming Foreign Minister in 1932. Those who had to deal with him found him sinister, inclined to be devious, and given to backstairs intrigue. He cared little for the League of Nations because it concerned itself with matters that Beck considered strictly internal concerns. The League's preoccupation with minorities, of which Poland had its share, was particularly vexing to Beck; the League's supervision of Danzig as a free city he considered an insult to Poland. He had never cared for the alliance with

France—perhaps because, earlier in his career, he had been expelled from France for trying to sell French military secrets. Beck longed for Poland to play the role of a big power, so he exaggerated Polish strength to the outside world. However, geography had played a trick on Poland; situated between Soviet Russia and Nazi Germany, a policy of independence—even of independence from France—would be difficult, if not impossible. The prospect of Germany and Soviet Russia coming to terms seemed impossible to Beck because of the great ideological gap between the two nations. But neither could he believe that Hitler would move against a nation courageous enough to fight. "Hitler," Beck told American ambassador William Bullitt in 1939, "was a timid Austrian who would not risk war against determined and strong opponents." [1]

In January 1938, when Beck became aware of Hitler's intention to destroy Austrian independence, he intimated to Hitler that Poland would not oppose *Anschluss,* hoping that Hitler would purchase Polish neutrality by solving the Danzig question. Hitler, however, ordered his troops into Austria without meeting Beck's price. Even though the deal over Austria fell through, Beck did not shrink from conniving with Hitler in the September crisis, because he considered Czechoslovakia to be an "artificial creation" [2] that was doomed to disappear. Both men agreed at that time that Czechoslovakia might become a "hotbed of bolshevism." [3] It was then also that Hitler hinted to Beck that Czechoslovakia would soon follow Austria into the Nazi empire. This news was not unpleasing to Beck who dreamed of founding a "Third Europe": a bloc of states, led by Poland and Hungary, stretching from the Baltic to the Adriatic. Because an independent Czechoslovakia blocked Beck from this goal, he joined Hit-

[1] Bullitt to Hull, April 7, 1939, *Foreign Relations of the United States, 1939,* I, pp. 117–119.
[2] Beck to Lipski, September 19, 1938, *Diplomat in Berlin, 1933–1939, Papers and Memoirs of Jozef Lipski* (New York, 1968), p. 406.
[3] Neurath memorandum, January 14, 1938, *Documents on German Foreign Policy,* Series D, V, p. 39.

ler in dissolving Czechoslovakia, with the hope that Slovakia and Ruthenia would not come under German domination.

Beck's policies during the Czechoslovak crisis seemed to reassure Hitler that, in return for Teschen, Poland would accept a position as a German satellite. If that sop proved insufficient to tame Poland, Hitler had no doubt that the Poles would understand the lesson to be learned from Czechoslovakia's fate—that Britain and France could not be relied upon to fight to uphold the Versailles treaty.

While the Munich victory was still fresh, the German campaign against Poland got underway, but only as a sideshow intended to divert Beck from his "Third Europe" idea. In October 1938, Beck sought to have Poland arbitrate the Hungarian demands on Czechoslovakia. The appearance of Poland as an arbiter in eastern Europe could have an unpleasant result for German interests—an increase in Polish prestige in an area now considered a German sphere of influence.

Consequently, on October 24, when Jozef Lipski, the Polish ambassador, argued heatedly in favor of Polish arbitration, Ribbentrop brought up the question of Danzig and the Polish Corridor. "Danzig was German—had always been German, and would always remain German," Ribbentrop declared to Lipski.[4] He proposed that Danzig come under German rule, and a German railroad and highway with extraterritorial rights be constructed across the Polish Corridor to Danzig. Further, Germany and Poland would guarantee their frontiers; and Poland would join the Anti-Comintern Pact, placing itself in opposition to Soviet Russia. If accepted, these demands would symbolize Polish commitment to Hitler's cause. In effect Poland would cease being a free agent and quietly become a German satellite.

By introducing the question of Danzig and the Corridor at this time, Ribbentrop was really seeking to forestall any Polish intervention in the Czechoslovak–Hungarian affair. However, as a result of the Munich settlement, Hitler sincerely believed that

[4] Memorandum by Hewel, October 24, 1938, in *ibid.*, pp. 105–106.

it would be possible to persuade the Poles to accept changes in the status of Danzig and the Corridor. But the Poles saw what Ribbentrop was hinting at, and so they dropped the subject. By the time Lipski next met with Ribbentrop on November 19, Ciano and Ribbentrop had succeeded in settling the Czechoslovak–Hungarian dispute themselves.

That left Beck faced with an unpleasant German proposal about Danzig and the Corridor. Lipski reported that Beck had rejected the October 24 proposal concerning German right to Danzig, and he submitted a counter-proposal, offering to expand the 1934 non-aggression pact and to replace the League of Nations guarantee of Danzig's international status with a Polish-German guarantee. Beck implied that any attempt at incorporating Danzig into Germany would lead to war. Ribbentrop accepted the Polish rejection good-naturedly, assuring Lipski that Germany wanted as good relations with Poland as possible; all of his efforts were directed towards that goal. Ribbentrop was surprised, he claimed, that Beck considered Hitler's proposals harmful to Polish–German relations and asked that Beck reconsider them for they were intended only to remove points of friction between the two countries.

But, throughout the following months, Beck would not budge, because he knew that these concessions would spell the end of Polish independence. Beck, however, had not learned from the example of Czechoslovakia. He imagined that obstinacy could be a substitute for guns and tanks. He did not believe that Hitler would dare to go to war. To the contrary, Hitler began moving toward forceful take-over when, on November 24, he issued a revised directive ordering preparations for a surprise occupation of Danzig whenever a suitable occasion appeared. Faced with a *fait accompli*, the Poles would speak less bravely.

Meanwhile, "negotiations" would continue. Beck wangled a personal meeting with Hitler on January 5, 1939; and the Fuehrer, not yet ready to give Beck the treatment he had given

Schuschnigg and Hacha, was on his best behavior. Hitler conceded that a strong Poland was necessary for Germany because of the Russian danger, but he insisted that Danzig was a German city and must be returned to the Reich. Hitler indicated that he was prepared to guarantee Poland's frontiers, including the Polish Corridor, but Beck was willing only to promise a continuation of the existing policy of avoiding dependence on Soviet Russia. As for Danzig, Beck stalled for more time; it was a difficult question, and he had to think of Polish public opinion.

On the second day of the meeting, Ribbentrop repeated the October demands, but Beck would concede nothing. He asked Ribbentrop to inform Hitler that there were no grounds for an agreement. Ribbentrop, however, assured Beck that Germany would not resort to force because it wanted friendly relations with Poland. Beck then left Berlin without an agreement and without concessions, but he left negotiations open. The last attempt at persuasion made by Ribbentrop was when he visited Beck in Warsaw on January 25 through 27. Although Beck refused all of Ribbentrop's proposals over Danzig, there was still no break in relations. Ribbentrop did not force the issue, and Beck did not reject further discussion.

Although he did not reveal the content of these talks to London and Paris, nevertheless, the rumor soon appeared that Beck had made a deal with Hitler. And Beck did not attempt to correct the misapprehensions: he kept silent lest Britain and France pressure him into concessions as they had done with Benes. By remaining silent yet rejecting Hitler's demands, Beck hoped to be able to settle the German–Polish problem without war and at the same time avoid a Munich-type conference over Poland.

When, on March 15, German troops occupied Bohemia and Moravia, Beck at first did not seem alarmed that German troops were dangerously near Polish borders, and he complained only about German machine guns being trained on Polish territory. He claimed to be happy over the "independence" of Slovakia and hoped that events of March 15 would aid Polish–German relations. But his elation could not obscure the ominous presence of German troops, which now flanked Poland on three sides. He did not hesitate to protest the establishment of a German protectorate over Slovakia—a major blow to his scheme for a Third Europe.

A new threat to European stability appeared when Viorel Tilea, the Rumanian minister, informed Halifax on March 17 of the imminent German aggression against Rumania. He explained that, in the course of economic negotiations, the German delegation had handed his government an ultimatum demanding a monopoly of Rumanian exports and a restriction on Rumanian production that would be favorable to German interests, in return for which Germany promised to "guarantee" the Rumanian frontiers. Tilea begged for British aid if Rumania should become a victim of German aggression. At any moment, he explained, German troops might attack. He thought the situation might be saved "if it was possible to construct a solid block of Poland, Rumania, Greece, Turkey, Yugoslavia with the support of Great Britain and France." [5]

Although Tilea's story was exaggerated, it contained enough truth to alarm Chamberlain and Halifax. Germany intended the German–Rumanian economic agreement to be the foundation of a German sphere of influence in southeastern Europe involving not only Rumania, but also Yugoslavia, Bulgaria, Hungary, and Turkey. But there were also political goals, according to Helmut Wohltat, who negotiated for Germany: "The political development of the national states in southeastern Europe will follow the German pattern to an increasing extent, while the influence of western European democracies and the Soviet Union would be eliminated." [6]

[5] Halifax to Hoare, March 17, 1939, *Documents on British Foreign Policy*, Third Series, IV, p. 367.
[6] Wohltat to Wiehl, February 27, 1939, *Documents on German Foreign Policy*, Series D, V, p. 407.

The British Foreign Office responded on March 18 by asking Warsaw, Ankara, Athens, Belgrade, Paris, and Moscow what their attitude would be should Rumania suffer German aggression. Only Paris would promise help. In Moscow, Litvinov disdained to share his opinion, but asked for a conference in Bucharest to discuss the possibilities of common action before the event. Halifax refused to send a cabinet minister halfway across Europe for a time-consuming conference when there seemed to be no assurance of success.

Suddenly faced with Tilea's story, Chamberlain was spurred on to a new foreign policy, which he considered to be necessary before negotiations could be resumed with Hitler. What Chamberlain called a "pretty bold and startling plan"[7] involved a declaration by Poland, France, Britain, and the Soviet Union that, whenever the political independence of any European nation was threatened, the four governments would consult on action to resist the threat. Chamberlain intended this declaration to force Hitler to desist from further aggression and return to the conference table. It would also encourage the small states, when threatened with aggression, to refuse to make the concessions that Hitler demanded. While this "new" policy was still not strong enough to deter Hitler, Chamberlain considered it radical because Britain was making a promise in advance. But the proposal was a bluff. Chamberlain did not believe that military action would ever be required. The promise, he thought, would be sufficient to make Hitler back down.

This proposed declaration was not to Beck's liking. Still hopeful of keeping Hitler contented, the Polish Foreign Minister scorned any public declaration made in association with the Soviet government because Berlin might interpret such a statement as proof that Poland had joined the Soviet camp. Instead, fearing that once the British and French were aware of Hitler's demands they would pressure him to concede as they had done

[7] Keith Feiling, *Neville Chamberlain* (London, 1946), p. 401.

with Czechoslovakia, Beck insisted on a secret bilateral treaty with Britain, while concealing the German demands from London. The bilateral agreement was not to Halifax's liking; he and Chamberlain preferred an arrangement in which Britain and France would come to the aid of Poland and Rumania—provided Poland and Rumania would aid each other and keep London and Paris informed on all developments that threatened their independence. Before this proposal could be acted on, Hitler moved again.

In the spring of 1939, after having spent a winter trying to decide whether to move east or west, Hitler again made a move toward achieving an "understanding" with Poland. He still wanted Danzig, but he had now added a demand for the Polish Corridor to his requirements of Polish subservience.

Seeking to capitalize on the occupation of Czechoslovakia, on March 21, Ribbentrop repeated his earlier demands to Jozef Lipski, but this time the friendly attitude was missing. Ribbentrop reported that Hitler was astounded by Poland's attitude, and suggested tactfully that Poland's salvation required a more friendly policy toward Germany.

While Lipski was in Warsaw conferring with Beck, Hitler was not idle. On March 23, Germany and Rumania signed the trade treaty, Slovakia officially became a German protectorate, and German troops occupied Memel, the chief port of Lithuania, which had been a German city before the Versailles treaty. This capitulation came about as a result of threats from Ribbentrop that Lithuania would fare better from a peaceful solution to its territorial dispute than from a military one; Lithuania agreed to evacuate the territory. Clearly, the move was intended to frighten the Poles, for Britain and France had no vital interest in Memel, and Germany could easily have recaptured the territory at any time. It succeeded in its intent: the Warsaw government was alarmed, immediately calling up reservists, while Polish newspapers attacked Beck for his shortsightedness in dealing with Hitler, and critics in parliament joined in the assault.

Faced with such opposition, Beck dared not seek accommodation with Hitler.

On March 25, Hitler had not yet fully made up his mind about Poland, according to a memorandum of a talk the Fuehrer had with General Brauchitsch. Hitler wanted a military solution of the Danzig question only if Poland would not cede it voluntarily; and he still clung to the hope that Beck would fall into line, for he wished to avoid pushing Poland into the arms of Britain. If he had to resort to a military solution, then a "coup" would have to be planned that would present the world with a *fait accompli*. Hitler ordered work on the final solution of the Polish problem to begin, with the instruction that "Poland would have to be so beaten down that during the next few decades, she need not be taken into account as a political factor." [8]

But the Memel coup had frightened the Warsaw government into believing that Danzig would be next. Under these circumstances, a hard-line policy was necessary to keep Hitler in check. He must understand that Poland would fight over Danzig.

When Lipski returned to Berlin on March 26 with Beck's answer to the demands made on March 21, he received a cold reception from Ribbentrop. Beck, so he reported, was willing to study improvement in transportation between Germany and East Prussia, but Germany could have no extraterritorial rights in the Polish Corridor. Beck was agreeable to a Polish–German guarantee of Danzig. Unhappy because there had been no move toward concession, Ribbentrop retorted that a settlement was possible only on a basis of the German demands, and that there could be no counter-proposals.

On March 28, caught between Hitler's inflexible demands and the mounting pressure from the Polish patriots, Beck warned Berlin that any German change in the administration of Danzig would be considered reason enough for Poland to go to war.

[8] Hitler's directive to the Commander-in-Chief of the Army, March 25, 1939, *Documents on German Foreign Policy*, Series D, VI, p. 117.

In London, the rumors of imminent war between Germany and Poland prodded Halifax and Chamberlain into action. Twice Halifax announced to the Polish ambassador that if the Danzig question became a threat to Polish independence, "His Majesty's Government would have to treat it as a question which was of the gravest concern to themselves." [9] By March 27, Halifax and Chamberlain extracted a pledge from the cabinet to promise aid to Poland and Rumania if either were in danger of German aggression, provided each assisted the other. Then Ian Colvin, a correspondent of the *London News Chronicle,* newly returned from Germany, came to the Foreign Office at the urging of the British military attaché in Berlin with an alarming story. His German contacts had indicated to him that Hitler intended to use the Danzig and Corridor problems to march on Poland at any time; and they claimed that only a public warning from Britain would deter him. Halifax had Colvin repeat his tale to Chamberlain. Imagining that they faced another *Anschluss,* Halifax and Chamberlain decided that now a swift, clear warning to Hitler was essential. This warning should take the form of a public pledge by Britain and France to support Poland if its independence were threatened.

Although their information did not indicate an impending coup, the Daladier government reluctantly agreed to the pledge, and it was presented to Beck. Faced with a proposal for a British and French guarantee, Beck pondered briefly and then accepted. He had not wanted this originally, but Hitler's demands, combined with the other pressures he faced—the activities of the Danzig Nazis, the Memel coup, and the pressure from within Poland to resist Hitler—led him finally to accept the pledge.

As a result of a peculiar series of decisions, the impossible had become fact: a British government had committed itself to intervene in Central Europe. On March 31, in response to a

[9] Halifax to Kennard, March 21, 1939, *Documents on British Foreign Policy,* Third Series, IV, p. 436.

question about the European situation, Chamberlain announced to the House of Commons that the government believed any question could be solved by peaceful means. But, in order to make the government's position perfectly clear, he declared:

. . . in the event of any action which clearly threatened Polish independence, and which the Polish government accordingly considered it vital to resist with their national forces, His Majesty's government would feel themselves bound at once to lend the Polish government all support in their power.[10]

Chamberlain's statement, often described as a revolution in British foreign policy, was actually more a revolution in tactics than in policy. During the Czechoslovak crisis, Britain had given no specific pledge to aid Czechoslovakia directly, but their intervention then had depended on France first becoming involved in a war. Chamberlain still believed Hitler could be brought to the conference table. Surely, a definite warning of British intention to support Poland, given in advance, would make Hitler pause, reflect on the consequences, and then return to peaceful negotiations.

Intending the pledge to function only as a temporary warning until some more permanent policy could be instituted, neither the Prime Minister nor Halifax expected it ultimately to involve Britain in a war over Poland. For they did not realize that, by promising help to Poland, Britain had challenged Hitler in what he considered to be his own backyard, where he could not tolerate such defiance. Ultimately, he would be forced to call the bluff.

To prevent Beck from considering this pledge a blank check to make unlimited demands on Britain whenever he wished, Halifax and Chamberlain did take steps. They requested that Beck keep London and Paris fully informed and that he refrain from any action that might antagonize Hitler.

However, Chamberlain and Halifax were still living in a

[10] *Parliamentary Debates, House of Commons*, Fifth Series, vol. 345, col. 2415.

world that had not existed since 1914. In 1939, the only kind of warning that would have been effective would have been guns and tank formations drawn up on the frontiers of Germany, with squadrons of heavy, long-range bombers loaded for attacks on German industrial centers. Hitler knew that British troops were few—and those in service were far from Germany—and that guns, tanks, and bombers had yet to be built. Words spoken in the House of Commons would have little effect on Adolf Hitler.

Part of Chamberlain's reasoning for making this public warning was that he hoped to avoid a misunderstanding similar to the one that he imagined had developed in July and August of 1914. Then, according to Chamberlain's version of history, Sir Edward Grey, the British Foreign Secretary, had failed to clarify Britain's intention to stand by France if Germany should launch an invasion. If Grey had spoken earlier and more clearly, Chamberlain believed that Germany would not have invaded France and Belgium.

In evaluating Chamberlain's intentions, however, Hitler was guided more by Britain's past inaction than by the speech in Commons. The Czechoslovak crisis had convinced him that British promises were made for home consumption and were never meant to be kept. Consequently, on April 3, he proceeded to order plans for the invasion of Poland, to be ready for execution by September 1, 1939. A directive dated April 11 contained the basic principles for *Operation White* and outlined the tasks for the Wehrmacht. Hitler stressed surprise attack, speed, and the swift annihilation of the Polish forces in order to present Britain and France with a *fait accompli.*

Beck still hoped to be able to settle with Hitler by himself, and so he trifled with the British. When he conferred with Chamberlain and Halifax on April 4 and 5, he was agreeable to a reciprocal aid arrangement between Poland and Britain, but he rejected Polish aid for other nations in Central Europe.

Determined to break through Hitler's unwillingness to negotiate, Beck now sought intermediaries, including the Japanese ambassador, to carry his pleas to Hitler. Through friendly diplomats, a meeting was arranged between Hans-Adolf von Molkte, the German ambassador, and Miroslaw Arciszewski of the Polish Foreign Ministry. Arciszewski reported Beck's denial that Poland had any intention of encircling Germany and claimed that he had been forced into the reciprocal arrangement with the British by public opinion. Anyway, he insisted, there was no way that it could conflict with the Polish–German non-aggression pact: it had been to insure this that he had refused Soviet membership in the arrangement.

Hitler responded by publicly denouncing the non-aggression pact, claiming that the Anglo-Polish arrangements had nullified it. On the same day, April 28, he confessed to the Reichstag that he had never considered the Munich Agreement as final. Further, to frighten the appeasers, he announced the end of the Anglo-German Naval Agreement of 1935. Danzig, he declared, would never become Polish; rightfully, to remove a danger to world peace, it ought to be returned to Germany.

Again, his speech was intended for foreign consumption; he hoped that his threats would have the same effect they had in the Czechoslovak affair. If he bullied enough, Britain and France would again push Germany's weak opponent into concessions, and he would intensify his pressure on Poland until Britain and France renounced their pledges of support, thereby leaving Germany completely free to have its way. But Hitler failed to realize that Beck was not Benes, and that the political repercussions of September 1938 would make Chamberlain avoid the same mistakes he had made with Czechoslovakia.

As a further move to dishearten his opponents, Hitler joined with Mussolini in the Pact of Steel, signed on May 22. Both Italy and Germany promised full aid to the other in a war, regardless of the circumstances under which the war began. Even if Germany were the aggressor, Italy was obligated to help. Nothing hid the offensive spirit of this pact, and Hitler spared nothing to give the signing the widest publicity. Mussolini, hoping that the

Pact would have an effect on his feud with France, joined under the impression that there would be no general war immediately.

The next day, Hitler informed his senior officers that Germany would attack Poland at the first suitable opportunity. He confessed that it was not Danzig that was at stake, but rather the domination of Poland; actually, war was necessary in order to expand German territory. However, he knew that he could not hope for the easy time they had in the Czechoslovak crisis; there would have to be some fighting, but they should be able to avoid a general war. Even if this did bring about a war with the western powers, he was convinced that this was the time to destroy Poland; because, in a war with Britain and France, Poland would be a danger at Germany's back.

Much of his speech to his officers dealt with the problem of Britain, whom he considered his chief enemy—for he had perceived that Britain led France. For this reason, preparations must be made for a war with Britain. They did not have to occupy themselves with Russia, he insisted, for Russia would not be likely to object to the liquidation of Poland. He hinted that an occupation of Belgium and Holland would eventually become necessary in order to secure them as bases for an attack on Britain. All efforts must be directed towards a short war, but they must nevertheless be prepared for a long one, perhaps one of ten or fifteen years' duration.

This conference indicates that Hitler had at last made up his mind. Poland could exist only on his terms; otherwise, there would be war. Hitler was not bluffing. His audience included officers upon whose help and professional advice he must depend for the carrying out of his plans. They could not be fooled; he must tell them the truth—not all, but enough to prepare them for war. He had revealed much of his thinking about the future; already he was contemplating attacking Belgium and Holland.

His audience got the message. By June 15, he had received the army's plan of operation against Poland, setting August 20 as the target date for completing Germany's preparations for war.

After that date, Hitler need only give the final order for the attack on Poland.

APPEASEMENT FAILS

While the German general staff labored over plans to wipe out Poland, German diplomats followed their instructions to denounce Anglo-French support for the Poles. Because of their March 31 declaration, the British received special attention. The Germans insinuated that Britain would be responsible for a general war, that it was Britain's backing of the Poles that was preventing Germany from settling the Danzig question peacefully. They insisted that Britain must withdraw their promise of aid to Poland.

However, it seemed publicly that the British government was determined to stop Hitler. Chamberlain announced to the House of Commons on April 13 that the government had given Greece and Rumania promises of help similar to that given Poland on March 31. Daladier joined in the pledge on the same day. Chamberlain informed the House of Commons on May 12 of an agreement with Turkey wherein both governments promised aid to each other in the event of war in the Mediterranean area. On April 26, he announced the introduction of conscription for military service, the first time in British history that it would be in effect in peacetime.

Despite these signs, Chamberlain continued to search for a peaceful solution of the Polish crisis, publicly denying at every opportunity that there was an attempt at encirclement of Germany. To show his good intentions, he handed over to Germany the Czechoslovak gold that had been held in the Bank of England. Both Halifax and Chamberlain repeatedly declared that the government would back a settlement of the Polish–German dispute as long as it was arrived at by discussion; and they strongly denied that Britain had any intention of standing in the way of German economic expansion in southeastern Europe. To reinforce this outward pressure, the British, in secret meetings with German representatives, proposed economic arrangements with Germany over southeastern Europe and agreements over armaments and colonies. Sir Horace Wilson even proposed a non-aggression pact and suggested that, if all these could be achieved, Britain would be able to evade the March 31 pledge to Poland. However, the Polish problem would not be solved. The use of an Anglo-German non-aggression pact as bait led Hitler to assume that Chamberlain was still so over-anxious about war that he would surrender rather than fight for Poland.

But Chamberlain's search for an arrangement with Hitler was complicated by a new force in Britain. Opposition to appeasement had become louder; and voices in the House of Commons were beginning to condemn Chamberlain's policy.

In the Czechoslovak crisis, the Soviet Union had lent assistance to Germany by keeping silent, but the isolation of Poland would require an agreement between Moscow and Berlin. Although Hitler's loud opposition to bolshevism had helped bring him to power, German army officers and diplomats favored an agreement with the Soviet Union. Despite their ideological differences, Soviet spokesmen had, throughout the years since 1933, hinted at their interest in friendly relations with Germany. They knew that rearmament during the Weimar period could not have been achieved with such speed had it not been for the Russian help. Furthermore, the two nations had common interests that had often been overlooked: they both shared a hatred for the Versailles settlement, and they both had old scores to settle with Poland.

The initiative for an agreement between the two countries was to come from Stalin. On March 10, 1939, before the Eighteenth Party Congress, he condemned Britain and France for rejecting collective security and accused them of seeking to bring about a war between Germany and the U.S.S.R. Purposely omitting the usual denunciation of nazism, he made Britain and France the targets of his invective. His concluding words were intended for Berlin:

We stand for peaceful, close and friendly relations with all neighboring countries which have common frontiers with the U.S.S.R. . . . We shall adhere to this position as long as these countries maintain like relations with the Soviet Union, and as long as they make no attempt to trespass, directly or indirectly, on the integrity and inviolability of the frontiers of the Soviet state.[11]

Stalin's statement was not a revolution in Soviet foreign policy, but it was simply a restatement of his old hope—agreement with Germany over eastern Europe. But from Berlin, there was only silence. Hitler had not only missed the significance of the speech, but more important, at the time of Stalin's feeler, he had not yet decided to change his policy and settle with Poland on the battlefield. Moscow had to take the initiative again. Alexei Merekalov, the Russian ambassador, who had not visited the German Foreign Ministry since presenting his credentials in June 1938, brought a message from the Kremlin on April 17. Ostensibly, the reason for the meeting was to discuss Soviet contracts with the Skoda works in Czechoslovakia for war materials. However, Merekalov proceeded to lead Ernst von Weizsaecker, the state secretary, into a discussion of German-Polish relations and finally came around to the subject of Russo-German affairs. Then Merekalov got to the point: ideological differences, he suggested, need not be a "stumbling block" to friendly relations. "Soviet Russia had not exploited the present friction between Germany and the western democracies against us [Germany], nor did she desire to do so." [12] There was no reason for Russia and Germany not to enjoy normal relations. Merekalov's statement was the first in a series of hints the Rus-

[11] *The Foreign Policy of the Soviet Union*, ed. by Alvin Z. Rubenstein (New York, 1960), p. 142.
[12] Weizsaecker memorandum, April 17, 1939, *Nazi-Soviet Relations* (New York, 1948), p. 2.

sians were to drop in the next six weeks; but, for the moment, Berlin chose not to pick up the hints.

Meanwhile, Britain and France were embarking on tortuous negotiations with the Soviet government. On April 14, the British pressed the Soviet Union to make a broad declaration promising to protect any neighbor who should resist aggression. Twenty-four hours after Merekalov had appealed to Weizsaecker for more normal relations, Maxim Litvinov replied to the British request by demanding a mutual assistance pact with a written guarantee of Russia's western neighbors—even if assistance were not requested—and a military convention. Litvinov scorned London's vague declaration, claiming it would invite a German attack on the Soviet Union. Should Soviet neighbors open their frontiers to Germany (as had Hacha), Russian soldiers would be forced to fight Germans on Russian borders. Litvinov's preference was for intervention in these nations before they had been occupied by Germany.

The British government, however, continued to press for a temporary pledge, in hopes of simply deterring Hitler until he decided to reform and return to the conference table. They considered the Soviet proposal an alliance for war, and they were reticent about forcing aid on unwilling nations. Litvinov's proposals required intense, detailed, and time-consuming negotiations; London favored less complicated and more practical measures. A mutual assistance pact might alarm Poland and Rumania, push them into the German sphere, hasten the division of Europe into armed camps, and provoke Hitler into some new rash act. Moreover, there was no assurance that the British public would go along with the idea of a pact with the Bolsheviks.

Like Hitler, Stalin continued to have doubts about British and French willingness to fight. His agents were fishing around for assurances that they—particularly the British—would stand up to Hitler. On the morning of May 3, British Ambassador William Seeds assured Litvinov that Britain would go to war to help any nation to whom promises had been made. This news must have cheered Stalin, for he had feared that the British and French might go back on their promises if the country to be defended should surrender quickly or be defeated, thereby leaving the Soviet Union faced with German armies on the Soviet borders. If the British stood firm on their commitment, and if Hitler were faced with opposition on the west and on the east, Hitler would be most likely to move against the west, leaving Russia free. Best of all, this situation would force Hitler to seek a deal to keep Russia out of the conflict.

Later that same day, Litvinov, who had for so long been sounding the call for collective security, was suddenly dismissed from his post. He may have suggested this step himself, because his past actions and his Jewish ancestry were barriers to his negotiating any agreement with Germany. It is certain that he was not liquidated because of disloyalty, for he had served Stalin well, both protecting the Soviet Union and providing a moral front for Soviet foreign policy.

Litvinov's post was filled by V. M. Molotov, chairman of the powerful Politburo subcommittee on foreign affairs. However, the replacement did not alter the official Soviet attitude. Molotov continued the demands Litvinov had made for a mutual assistance pact. In negotiations with the Germans, both Litvinov and Molotov were considerate and polite while maintaining a tight security. In their dealings with the British and French, both were insulting, arrogant, and suspicious—Molotov a little more so than Litvinov, deliberately humiliating the ambassadors by seating them below him and making them use their laps for writing while he looked down from behind a desk. But actually, Molotov's external appearance was deceiving; in fact, Stalin's "trusted" aide was accompanied throughout the talks by a recording device that took down every word.

Because they needed Russia more than Russia needed them, the British and French governments eventually had to give in to Molotov's demands. Having pledged aid to Poland, Rumania, Turkey, and Greece, insuring that if Hitler started a war with one of them, he would also face war in the west, Britain and France needed Russian help to implement their promises, but help would not be given except on Moscow's terms. On May 24, the British and French finally informed the Kremlin that they would be willing to negotiate a mutual assistance pact. They drafted a treaty for Soviet consideration, requiring Soviet Russia to aid France and Britain if they became involved in a war with a European power that had attacked Britain and France or had attacked a nation to whom Britain and France had promised help. If Soviet Russia became involved in a war under similar circumstances, Britain and France would reciprocate.

As soon as it had been presented, Molotov found the Anglo-French concession unacceptable, claiming that the British and French were simply trying to drag out the talks and that they were really uninterested in being tied down by a concrete agreement. Protests by the French and British ambassadors had no effect on Molotov. "My words," British Ambassador Seeds complained, "seemed not to be heard or understood." [13] On another occasion, he observed, "It is my fate to deal with a man totally ignorant of foreign affairs and to whom the idea of negotiation—as distinct from imposing the will of his party leader—is utterly alien." [14]

Trying to pacify the Russians, Paris and London prepared a new draft, and Sir William Strang of the British Foreign Office was dispatched to help in the negotiations. But Strang's appointment was taken as proof of British insincerity. The Russians were insulted that no one of higher rank had been sent to negotiate. Had not Chamberlain himself journeyed three times to talk in person with Hitler? However, Chamberlain knew the Russians already had too many advantages, and to have sent a more important person would have seemed to be too conciliatory. London also feared the effect on Hitler if someone too important

[13] Seeds to Halifax, May 28, 1939, *Documents on British Foreign Policy,* Third Series, V, p. 711.
[14] Seeds to Halifax, May 30, 1939, *ibid.,* p. 722.

went to Moscow. The original plan had been to call Seeds back for consultation; but he was ill with the flu, and Strang's appointment made sense because he had served in the Moscow embassy and knew the Russian language.

Of course, Molotov found the new draft unacceptable. Molotov was dissatisfied with every Anglo-French proposal and always found new excuses for objections. He reflected his "sincerity" and that of his government by demanding immediate concessions and by jumping from one complaint to another without reason. He avoided any measure that might have speeded up the negotiations and further delayed matters by insisting on detailed proposals that would require prolonged study. He always demanded more than he thought anyone would reasonably agree to, hoping that the British and French would break off the talks; but London and Paris were under pressure from home to continue the negotiations, and so did not fall into that trap.

But the Germans were presented with a different face. Soviet chargé Georgei Astakov, on May 17 in a conversation with Karl Schnurre of the German Foreign Ministry, asserted that there were no foreign-policy conflicts between their two nations. As for the Anglo-Soviet negotiations, Schnurre was assured, "the result desired by England would hardly be achieved." [15]

The negotiations over the political arrangements for the mutual assistance pact finally ground to a halt in late July. The British and French had no choice but to reject the Molotov doctrine of "indirect aggression," which would involve the guaranteeing of states, with or without their consent, against surrender to Hitler's threats. Under the guise of forestalling German occupation, Stalin had asked for an Anglo-French blessing to Russian occupation of Turkey, Greece, Rumania, Poland, Estonia, Latvia, and Finland if necessary, but the British and French would not buy it.

With the negotiations over political arrangements at a stand-

---

[15] Schnurre memorandum, May 17, 1939, *Nazi–Soviet Relations* (New York, 1948), p. 5.

still, Molotov switched his argument to ask for an immediate military convention. Although London and Paris preferred the accustomed procedure of military talks conducted after the political agreement had been signed, Molotov was adamant about adjourning the political talks for extensive discussions concerning every type of military assistance—including land, sea, and air. London and Paris knew that these talks would require months to complete, but they gave in.

The military talks began on August 12, but soon stalled over the question of the weaker nations along the Soviet frontiers. Britain and France wanted to send armed help only if invited, but the Russians did not want to wait for an invitation. They argued that, to avoid having to fight Germany across Poland and Rumania, Soviet generals had to have some assurance of peaceful passage. With Beck refusing permission, knowing that the unity of Poland would not long survive a Russian occupation, the negotiations could move no further.

The Soviet delegation, headed by Marshal Kliment E. Voroshilov, contemptuously referred to the British and French governments as the "yielding powers," and presented their delegation with the Russian "demands (not requests) . . . somewhat in the manner of a victorious power dictating terms to a broken enemy." [16] Voroshilov castigated the British and French governments for failing to give their delegations plenipotentiary power, but he himself had not been given it. Whenever a definite decision was needed, he had to recess the meeting and hurry away to confer with Stalin. On August 17, Voroshilov adjourned the conference temporarily until the British and French delegations could obtain answers from their governments to the "cardinal question": would Russian troops be permitted to pass through Poland and Rumania to make contact with enemy troops? Without this concession, Voroshilov declared, the Soviet Union could give no help to Britain and France. (In the political

[16] Drax to Chatfield, August 16, 1939, *Documents on British Foreign Policy,* Third Series, VII, p. 33.

negotiations, Litvinov and Molotov had both neglected to bring up this "cardinal question," which Voroshilov now considered essential to any military negotiations.) On August 21, while the British and French delegations were still consulting their governments, Voroshilov postponed the meetings indefinitely, with the lame excuse that the Russian generals had to be with their troops on maneuvers. The meetings were never resumed, although on August 22 the French government instructed the head of the French delegation to sign whatever terms he could get for a military convention that would include agreement to the passage of Soviet troops through Poland after the outbreak of war. Voroshilov refused further discussions, using the excuse that the British and Polish governments had not yet given their consent to the passage of troops.

London and Paris were later to be criticized for failing to accommodate the Soviet government at this time; but even if they had been able to overcome all their objections, Molotov would have been forced to devise other roadblocks. It is to its credit that the Chamberlain government refused to purchase Soviet aid at such a price. Chamberlain, it is true, was suspicious of the Russians. But critics of his government have too readily accepted the sincerity of Moscow, forgetting that Stalin had been seeking an arrangement with Hitler since 1933. There is no indication that Moscow was sincere in the negotiations. To the contrary, the constant faultfinding by the Soviet negotiators, the criticism of Britain and France by the Moscow press, the leakage of information about the talks by the Russians, and their sudden remembering of the "cardinal question," all point to a wish by the Soviet Union to sabotage the negotiations. Had the three governments feared Hitler as much in 1939 as they were to fear him later, an agreement might have been reached; but, as long as neither side believed Hitler to be dangerous enough to force a burial of their differences, agreement was impossible. Most important to remember, for the U.S.S.R., the more attractive offer —peace rather than war—was to come from Berlin.

Throughout June and July, Moscow and Berlin had been using their economic discussions as a blind to cover their explorations of mutual interests. Whenever German interest flagged, as it did from time to time because Hitler had not yet made up his mind, Moscow would arouse it, if not directly, then by some indirect means. On June 15, although the two men were scarcely acquainted, Astakov paid a visit to the Bulgarian minister in Berlin "without any apparent reason." After a long talk stretching over two hours, Astakov said, "If Germany would declare that she would not attack the Soviet Union or that she would conclude a non-aggression pact with her, the Soviet Union would probably refrain from concluding a treaty with England." [17] As Moscow had intended, these remarks were quickly reported to the German Foreign Ministry, but the Russians were not to confirm the promise by direct negotiations until August. By then, Soviet intelligence had learned about the German preparations for war, making it more pressing for Germany to make an agreement with Russia. Knowing they had the advantage over Berlin, Moscow applied further pressure by pursuing negotiations with Britain and France and carefully leaking details of the talks. By the end of July, however, Berlin had learned that the Anglo-French conversations with the Russians had ground to a halt and that the military talks would have little chance of success. At the same time, Sir Horace Wilson, speaking for Chamberlain, had approached Helmut Wohltat with the offer of an Anglo-German non-aggression pact, which would mean the isolation of Poland. These favorable signs seemed to indicate that it was time for Germany to take up the Russian offer.

Accordingly, on August 2, Ribbentrop offered the Russian chargé a deal. If Moscow would remodel Russo-German relations, he suggested that there would be "no problem from the Baltic to the Black Sea that could not be solved between the two of us." Russian interests in the Baltic did not have to clash

[17] Woermann memorandum, June 15, 1939, *Documents on German Foreign Policy*, Series D, VI, pp. 728–729.

with German. "In case of Polish provocation we would settle accounts with Poland in the space of a week."[18] He hinted at a possible Russo-German pact that would determine the fate of Poland. But Moscow did not reply. A week later, worried by the Russian silence, Berlin became more specific. Because war with Poland might soon be necessary, Germany was prepared to satisfy Russian interests in Poland; and, if war did come, there was certainly no need for a disagreement between Germany and Russia over Poland. Stalin was satisfied that he had Hitler where he wanted him; an answer arrived in Berlin within forty-eight hours, inviting an emissary to Moscow for consultations on the subject of Poland and Russian–German relations.

While this invitation was being considered, Ciano came to Germany for conferences with Ribbentrop and Hitler. Troubled over impending war, which Italy dreaded, Ciano had been instructed by Mussolini to discuss ways of avoiding war, for the Duce feared that a war over Poland could escalate into a world war. Ciano, however, found Hitler determined and very frank about his intentions. Poland had to be defeated, he declared, because it was a threat to Germany "in the inevitable clash with the western democracies."[19] Too many German divisions would have to be tied up watching Poland. But, Hitler assured Ciano, there was no immediate danger of world war; the western democracies would not be willing to commit themselves to anything so drastic. Therefore, he revealed, he had decided that a showdown with Poland was essential, and it would be up to Poland to decide whether or not fighting would occur. But, to Ciano's dismay, not only had Hitler decided upon a showdown, but he had decided on an immediate one. He would give Poland until August 31 to surrender. His reason was that any military campaign begun after that date might run over into the rainy season, which usually began in the middle of October. Even

[18] Ribbentrop to Schulenberg, August 3, 1939, in *ibid.*, p. 105.
[19] Schmidt memorandum, *Documents on German Foreign Policy*, Series D, VII, p. 42.

more dismayed than when he had arrived, Ciano returned to Rome, cursing Hitler for betraying Italy.

With time now growing short, negotiations with the Russians had to be speeded up. On August 14, in a message intended for Stalin, Ribbentrop took great pains to explain that there was no conflict of interest between Germany and Russia. Germany had no aggressive intentions against Russia; rather, the western democracies had tried to create that impression because they were seeking to lure Russia into a war against Germany, and such a fate had to be avoided. To save time, it was recommended that Ribbentrop go to Moscow, explain Hitler's views, and conclude a settlement.

That same day, a confident Hitler reviewed the political situation with his generals. He again discounted the possibility of Britain engaging in a war over Poland. Furthermore, he suggested, Britain lacked leadership. "The men I got to know in Munich are not the kind that start a new world war." He was also confident that France was uninterested in the events of eastern Europe, that Russia would stay out of the war, and that, without leadership, other European nations would seek neutrality. He knew that Anglo-French military forces were unprepared to face the armies of the new Germany. From tapped telephone conversations, he also knew that the British had been paving the way for him by trying to dampen the Poles' spirit. Already, he claimed, the British had put out feelers on his intentions for Europe after he had disposed of Poland. He expected Britain to make a show of resistance to "talk big, even recall her ambassador, perhaps put a complete embargo on trade, [but] she is sure not to resort to armed intervention in the conflict." [20]

However, the understanding with Soviet Russia, so essential to a German victory over Poland, was still to be worked out. Molotov also had some questions that had yet to be discussed. Would Germany be willing to conclude a non-aggression pact?

[20] Halder notebook, August 14, 1939, in *ibid.*, p. 555.

Hitler consented. How did he feel about a joint guarantee of the Baltic states? Hitler was willing. Would he use German influence to persuade Japan to improve relations with Russia? Again, yes. But Molotov wanted Germany to sign an economic agreement. With no other choice if his military schedule were to be met, Hitler obliged.

On August 19, Germany and the Soviet Union signed a trade agreement, by which the Russians were to receive a credit of 200 million Reichsmarks and were to supply the Germans with 100 million Reichsmarks' worth of raw materials during the following two-year period. The way seemed clear for a political agreement. But Molotov requested a lapse of one week before Ribbentrop would come to Moscow to complete the bargain, and that meant a week's delay in Hitler's timetable. Hitler had to resort to a personal message to Stalin in order to extract an invitation for Ribbentrop to come to Moscow sooner. Finally, Ribbentrop and Molotov signed the non-aggression pact in the evening of August 23, just one week short of Hitler's deadline.

The pact was to run for ten years. If one partner went to war, the other promised to remain neutral. Significantly, there was no escape clause automatically invalidating the pact if one member should launch an aggressive war. Thus, Stalin left Hitler free to attack Poland whenever he wished. A secret protocol, drafted in Moscow and accepted by Hitler, clinched the deal for Stalin: while Lithuania would belong in the German sphere of influence, Finland, Estonia, and Latvia would be in the Russian sphere; and Poland would be divided between Russia and Germany along the Narev, Vistula, and San rivers. Germany would recognize Russian interest in Bessarabia (then in Rumania), and would claim no part of southeastern Europe.

Hitler could now be certain that Stalin would not trouble him in the east while he attacked Poland and then turned his attention to Britain and France; and Stalin not only had peace but a promise of spheres of influence that Britain and France had denied him. (However, when the secret protocol was introduced in the Nuremberg trials, Soviet lawyers would denounce it as a forgery.)

Secure that the pact was to be signed the following day, Hitler called his senior commanders to an all-day conference on August 22 and announced to them that war with Poland must come in 1939, rather than later when conditions for war might not be so favorable for Germany. Now its enemies were unprepared for war. "There is no real armament in England, but only propaganda." France, short of men because of the declining birthrate, had done little to rearm. The most that could be expected from the West at this time would be a blockade of Germany, which would be ineffective, or an attack mounted from the Maginot Line, which was impossible, according to Hitler. "Now Poland is in the position in which I wanted her," Hitler gloated. "Our enemies are small fry. I saw them in Munich." In another speech that same day, Hitler exhorted his officers to wage a brutal, relentless war, with the objective: "The wholesale destruction of Poland." [21]

This was not the speech of a man who would consider pulling back from war at the last moment. Hitler had committed himself and Germany without reservation. Peace was no longer possible unless Poland capitulated. He could not turn back without endangering his regime, because the German officer corps had no scruples about a war with Poland. The next day, he ordered war to begin on August 26 at 4:30 AM.

Chamberlain continued to keep channels open to Berlin because he preferred a settlement to a war, but he dared not repeat his trips of the previous year even though hints had come from Berlin for a visit. Instead, having heard reports that German troops were concentrating for an invasion, Chamberlain resorted to a secret letter, sent to Hitler on August 22, attempting to convince Hitler that Britain would fight if German soldiers entered Poland.

[21] Memoranda on Hitler's speeches, August 22, 1939, in *ibid.*, Series D, VII, pp. 200–206.

In his letter, Chamberlain vowed that, despite the Nazi–Soviet pact, Britain would not step down from its obligations to Poland. Believing that war could have been avoided in 1914 if Britain had made its position clear, Chamberlain pointed out to Hitler that war between Britain and Germany would be a great calamity, and that there was nothing between Poland and Germany that could not be settled peacefully. He recommended a truce on both sides in order to settle minority problems, after which direct Polish–German discussions could begin.

When Neville Henderson, the British ambassador, presented the letter to Hitler on August 23, the Fuehrer went into one of his fits of rage. The British were preventing a settlement of the Polish question and preparing for war, he insisted, while Germany was only trying to defend itself. Thousands of Germans were being dragged off to Polish concentration camps, and the British had given the Poles a blank check for attacking Germany. The British would have to pay for this, he warned. He would not allow Germans to be slaughtered just to satisfy the whims of the British. If Poland made the slightest move against the Germans or against Danzig, Hitler intended to "intervene."

Later that day, still keeping to the theme of "perfidious Albion," Hitler handed Henderson a letter in which he swore that he had not sought any conflict with Britain, but that Danzig and the Corridor belonged in the German sphere of interest. Germany was prepared to settle these questions through negotiations, but the British pledge to Poland, coupled with allegations about German mobilization and German designs on other countries, had destroyed any Polish inclination to negotiate. Encouraged by the British, he insisted, the Poles had loosed a wave of terrorism against the Germans living in Poland, and Hitler would not tolerate these or further acts of provocation. Finally, if Britain and France carried out mobilization measures, he threatened to order the immediate mobilization of the Wehrmacht.

Unsaid but understood in Hitler's letter was the question, "Why fight for Poland?" He was striving to frighten the British—

and thereby the French—away from Poland; but London did not retreat. On August 24, Parliament assembled and heard declarations from Chamberlain and Halifax that the government would stand by Poland. That same day, Parliament voted an emergency powers bill giving the executive exceptional powers to take whatever steps were necessary in the event of war. Apparently the news of the Nazi–Soviet pact had not been awesome enough to alter the government's policies, so Hitler would have to do more to bring the British to desert Poland.

Hitler summoned Henderson to the Reichschancellery on August 25 and gave him an offer intended to be as decisive as that given Russia. Hitler indicated that he was prepared to make another offer to Britain after the German–Polish problem had been solved. He was willing to conclude an agreement that would "not only guarantee the existence of the British empire in all circumstances as far as Germany is concerned but would also if necessary assure the British empire of German assistance." [22] He claimed to be ready to accept a limitation on armaments and to be uninterested in altering the western frontiers of Germany.

Hitler also gave a "Why fight for Poland?" message to French Ambassador Robert Coulondre. The possibility that Germans and Frenchmen should spill their blood over Poles was dreadful; but Germany could not tolerate the Polish provocations much longer. Seventy thousand refugees had been forced to flee Poland; on the 24th, seven Germans had been shot; thirty German reservists had been machine-gunned; and Polish ships had fired on a German plane carrying a state secretary. Hitler implored the ambassador to give his message to Daladier quickly. He said: "I want to avoid a conflict. I will not attack France, but if she enters the war, I will carry on to the end." [23]

Later in the same day, Hitler telephoned Mussolini to tell him that an attack on Poland was imminent and that he needed

[22] Hitler to Henderson, August 25, 1939, in *ibid.*, p. 281.
[23] Coulondre to Bonnet, August 25, 1939, *Le livre jaune français* (Paris, 1939), p. 313.

the help that Mussolini had promised in the Pact of Steel. Faced with the message he had been dreading and with his armies not yet recovered from the Spanish Civil War, Mussolini had to yield to the pleadings of Ciano and confess to Hitler that Italy could not go to war unless he were furnished with urgently needed supplies.

Before receiving Mussolini's reply, Hitler confidently ordered the attack on Poland to begin the next day, August 26. Then, about 4:30 AM, the news reached Berlin that Britain and Poland had joined in an alliance, promising to support each other if attacked by an aggressor; in secret clauses, they indicated that Germany was the anticipated aggressor and that a threat to Danzig would be cause enough for invoking the alliance. Then came Mussolini's message that Italy would not come to his aid, destroying Hitler's hope that the Italian fleet would keep the British occupied with their Mediterranean communications. Hitler's confidence was badly shaken. About 7:30 PM, he canceled the order for war.

Hitler's decision resulted more from the Anglo-Polish alliance than from Mussolini's defection, because the alliance appeared to be a direct challenge. However, for the Chamberlain government, it was only another effort to shock Hitler into negotiating over Poland. For Hitler it meant that he must devote more time to isolating Poland from its new ally.

Early in the morning of August 27, Hitler was roused from his bed by Goering with the news that a Swedish businessman, Birger Dahlerus, who had acted as an intermediary between London and Berlin before, had brought a message from Halifax. Dahlerus reported that the British government needed time to consult with Henderson and to draft a reply to Hitler's latest proposal and that it was interested in solving the question that troubled the peace of Europe. Hitler replied with a rambling monologue on his early career and his troubles with the British. Then he questioned Dahlerus on life in Britain. Finally, Hitler stated his terms—Danzig and the Corridor, a guarantee of rights

for the Germans living in Poland, a German guarantee of the
Polish frontiers, return of the German colonies, and a pledge to
defend the British Empire. Furthermore, he insisted, he must
have a conference with British leaders, hinting at another Munich.

With patience, Hitler could have reached his goal. When
Chamberlain received Dahlerus' report, he seriously considered
the possibilities; he doubted if the Poles would be willing to concede all of the Corridor. At this time, Chamberlain would have
accepted the return of Danzig to Germany and the formation of
an extraterritorial road across the Corridor, which were the
original demands presented by Ribbentrop in October 1938.
Having worn down the British to this point in less than a year, it
is likely that, if Hitler had waited, he could have obtained all
his objectives this way.

His campaign to frighten the French brought a doleful message from Daladier on August 26. The premier assured Hitler
that German–Polish differences could be settled peacefully; but
he warned that, if there were a war bloodier than the last, the
only victors would be the "forces of destruction and barbar-
ism." [24] Hitler replied on August 27 with the accustomed story
of the iniquitous Treaty of Versailles and with a repetition of his
demand for Danzig and the Corridor. To his message, he added
a prophecy: if war should come, whatever the outcome, "the
Polish state of today would disappear in one way or another." [25]

By August 28, Hitler had developed a policy that he hoped
would isolate Poland in time for the war, which was now
planned for September 1. With the intention of driving a wedge
between the British and the Poles, he would force Poland into an
unfavorable position through demands for Danzig, the Corridor,
and a plebiscite. If he could get the British to accept his offer and
the Poles to reject it, then he would have his war only with Po-

[24] Daladier to Hitler, August 26, 1939, *Documents on German Foreign Policy,* Series D, VII, p. 331.
[25] Hitler to Daladier, August 27, 1939, in *ibid.,* p. 359.

land. By now, however, the pressures had begun to take their toll of Hitler; one of his aides reported him "exhausted, haggard, croaking voice, preoccupied." [26]

About 10:30 PM on August 28, Henderson, "fortified by a half bottle of champagne," [27] brought Chamberlain's message to Hitler. The Prime Minister recommended a settlement between Poland and Germany, to be guaranteed by other powers and to be undertaken by direct negotiations between Poland and Germany. He assured the Fuehrer that Beck was prepared to enter into such discussions. However, Beck's promise had not been secured without pressure. By August 29, Polish prospects were far from promising. German troops were moving into position along the Polish frontiers, and there were stories of Russian troop movements on the eastern borders of Poland. Rumors circulated about German units entering Slovakia. Beck wanted to proceed with general mobilization, but Sir Howard Kennard, the British ambassador, talked him into postponing it until London could receive Hitler's reply.

That evening about 7:15 PM, Henderson reported to the Reichschancellery, where he received a memorandum containing Hitler's response. After listing his complaints over the conduct of the Poles, which had finally forced him to safeguard German national interests, he announced that he was willing to accept the British proposal for direct negotiations if a Polish emissary was in Berlin by August 30 with full powers to negotiate. Hitler planned to use the tactics that had been so successful with Schuschnigg and Hacha: get one man into a position to make the decision, and then bully and threaten him until he would surrender his country entirely.

In passing Hitler's proposal on to Lipski, Henderson begged that it be accepted. Beck, he thought, would be just the man for the trip. However, remembering the examples of Schuschnigg

[26] Halder's notebook, August 28, 1939, in *ibid.*, p. 564.
[27] Henderson to Halifax, August 29, 1939, *Documents on British Foreign Policy*, Third Series, VII, p. 386.

and Hacha, the Polish government withstood the pleas. They preferred to fight rather than send Beck, or any other representative, to have to confront Hitler's bullying. On the morning of August 30, Poland ordered a general mobilization.

One delay after another prevented Henderson from conveying London's reply to Ribbentrop until about midnight on August 30. Henderson reported that Warsaw had been informed of Hitler's request, but the first step for any negotiation would have to be for Germany and Poland themselves to work out the arrangements. The British government found it impossible to have an emissary with the powers requested in Berlin as soon as August 30. In the meantime, some temporary arrangements should be worked out to try to ease the tensions. Henderson suggested that it might be helpful for Germany to follow the normal procedure of talking directly with the Polish ambassador and having him convey the German terms to Warsaw.

Almost as if he had not heard Henderson at all, Ribbentrop whipped out a document and proceeded to rattle off sixteen points demanded by Hitler. Henderson asked for a copy but Ribbentrop refused, explaining that, because the time limit for a Polish emissary to appear in Berlin had expired, the proposals were useless. Interpreting this as an ultimatum, the usually obsequious Henderson angrily turned on Ribbentrop. The argument between the two men became so heated that observers feared they might come to blows.

The terms read off by Ribbentrop were deceptively liberal. Danzig would be returned to Germany, but the fate of the Corridor would be determined by plebiscite conducted by an international commission. All Polish forces would have to evacuate the area immediately, but there should be a year's delay in the plebiscite (which would give the Nazis time to establish their hold on the area). Were Poland to win the plebiscite, Germany would have to be given an extraterritorial traffic zone across the Corridor. If Germany won, Poland would receive a similar right of access to the sea. Also, if the Corridor returned to Germany, an exchange of populations would be arranged to alleviate the minority problem; and an international commission would be created to examine all minority complaints, with both countries compensating for any damages. Both nations would enter into binding agreements to protect the minorities residing within their frontiers. And finally, once these agreements were accepted, Poland and Germany would demobilize their military forces.

Hitler hoped that the British would take the bait and the Poles would refuse it, thereby driving a wedge between Britain and Poland. He also intended that his proposals would serve as an alibi for the record—to make his case look good not only to the German people but to the rest of the world as well. In the evening of August 31, the terms were broadcast to the world as German soldiers took up their positions for the attack on Poland.

In the morning of August 31, Hitler issued the directive for war. In accordance with *Operation White,* hostilities would begin at 4:45 AM on September 1. Flights over neutral territory by the Luftwaffe were prohibited unless there were indications that large French and British formations were on the way, in which case, the Luftwaffe would counter enemy air attacks. If Britain and France did attack, German forces would remain on the defensive to make Britain and France appear responsible for war.

Meanwhile, the negotiations continued. Henderson had been prodding the Polish ambassador into inquiring officially about Hitler's terms, and Goering made certain that the terms were given to Dahlerus, who of course passed them on to the British embassy and to the Polish ambassador. As Hitler had hoped, the pressure was now on the Poles. In the afternoon of August 31, Beck gave in to the pressure from London and Paris and instructed Lipski to announce to Ribbentrop that Poland would exchange views directly with Germany on arrangements for future discussions. But Lipski would not be empowered to accept any document himself or to discuss Hitler's proposals. At 6:30 in the evening, Lipski reported to Ribbentrop, who asked if Lipski had been given the power to negotiate. After receiving the negative reply and after reminding Lipski that Hitler had asked for an emissary with full powers by August 30, Ribbentrop curtly ended the interview. When Lipski returned to the embassy, he found that the telephone lines to Warsaw had been cut and he had no way of communicating with his government.

To reinforce his case that the war was defensive, Hitler staged incidents along the German–Polish frontiers. Germans dressed in Polish uniforms fired a few shots and placed bodies of Gestapo prisoners dressed in German uniforms along the border as evidence of a Polish attack. Another detachment of German soldiers dressed as Poles entered a German radio station near Gleiwitz and broadcast in Polish a report of the "attack" on Germany.

Now, having established his case carefully to make it appear that he was complying with the terms of the Paris peace pact, Hitler had his troops cross the Polish borders the next morning, right on schedule. With Poland invaded on three sides in broad daylight and with the planes of the Luftwaffe bombing towns and railroads, the peace negotiated on November 11, 1918 had ended.

Before the cataclysm, however, there was one last-ditch effort at appeasement. Chamberlain proposed before Commons that, if Germany merely *agreed* to withdraw its troops from Poland (which was not the same as actually completing a withdrawal), then his government would consider that affairs were back to the status of August 31, before the invasion. Then, Britain would be prepared to join in a conference on the Polish–German problem.

However, the House of Commons and cabinet rebelled and forced Chamberlain to forsake his campaign for peace. At 11:00 AM on September 3, with no response from Berlin to London's demand that the invasion be halted, Britain went to war. France followed at 5:00 PM. Both countries were in a conflict they had never wanted and had labored to avoid. However, Hitler had been determined to have a war over Poland. Now he had it, although he had not wished to fight Britain and France at the same time.

CONCLUSION

The war that came to Europe in 1939 came because the only alternative for Hitler—when faced with a country that would not succumb to threats—was war. Hitler had promised to restore German territory to Germany and to restore Germany to its rightful place in the world. Poland had received German territory through the Treaty of Versailles. Therefore, Hitler could not back down from Poland; he had to proceed with his objectives, and the only thing that would be able to alter his course would be war.

Many political commentators since 1939 have claimed that, if nations had acted earlier, there would have been no war. If the League had fought Japan over Manchuria, they claim, or if the League had defended Ethiopia, in 1935, or if France and Britain had invaded the Rhineland in 1936, then Hitler could not have attacked Poland. But it would have been impossible for Britain and France to have entered any kind of war—offensive or defensive, small-scale or large-scale—before 1939, because neither the people nor the governments of the two countries were conditioned to the idea of war. The only way they could accept war after 1918 was for it to be thrust upon them by a series of crises, such as those that finally culminated in the German invasion of Poland. Arguments over when and where Hitler should have been halted, then, are purely academic, because before September 1, 1939 Hitler had done nothing that any major power considered dangerous enough to warrant precipitating a major European war.

Nor was there any existing coalition that could have opposed Hitler's massive forces. For Britain sought to appease Hitler, the French feared a repetition of the bloody sacrifices of 1914–1918, Stalin wanted an agreement with Hitler on partitioning Europe, and the United States rejected all responsibility for Europe. Peace would have been possible in 1939 only if there had existed a great military alliance, including both France and Britain, but headed by the United States and the Soviet Union, that was prepared to defend the governments of eastern Europe. But, until Hitler would force them into an alliance, capitalism and communism were prevented from cooperating to oppose nazism by their ideological differences, jealousies, suspicions, and power politics.

If, in 1919, Germany had been occupied and divided as it was to be in 1945, war might not have come about. Until the Germans were satisfied by revisions in the peace treaty, however, peace was definitely impossible. This brings up the question: would a fully rearmed Weimar Republic, then, have prevented war? Or would a strong, vigorous German Republic, with all of its territory restored, have initiated a conflict without Hitler? Probably not, but such a Germany would have been fully capable of dominating Europe as Hitler did, and a rearmed Weimar Republic would have been tempted to retrieve the lands taken away by the Treaty of Versailles.

Perhaps if the Treaty of Versailles had been strictly enforced, Europe might have been able to enjoy peace, but this required several impossibilities: the occupation of the Rhineland until 1935, strict execution of the disarmament provisions of the Treaty of Versailles, and, most important, a certain amount of wisdom in administering reparations payments. But these were made impossible by the cries of injustice both from within Germany and from the appeasers in the other treaty nations. The appeasers had as their objective the restoration of the Germany of 1914. But the Germany of 1914 had precipitated a world war; if that Germany were restored, would it again bring about a war? With the memory of the war still fresh in everybody's minds, the appeasers thought it unlikely—surely, having undergone such devastation, the Germans had learned their lesson.

Certainly, if it had been followed through to the fullest, appeasement would have prevented war, for the appeasers could have continued to surrender until there was nothing left to give. However, the treaty powers were willing to pay only so much and no more for peace. When Hitler achieved *Anschluss*, the balance of power shifted in Germany's favor, and it shifted even more when Czechoslovakia fell. But the appeasers no longer felt as generous as they had in the past. From this time forward, appeasement was on its way out. Hitler, feeling overconfident from his victory, did not realize that Britain was capable of any other policy but appeasement, and so believed he could take Poland without any interference.

So it was Hitler who was chiefly responsible for war, and he did not stumble into war with Poland by mistake. Hitler could not understand that events since September 1938 had so shaken British politicians that there had been a revolution in British politics. Tories, Liberals, and Laborites had finally become resolved to war. Hitler had forced unity on British opinion and had driven the House of Commons to rebel against appeasement. As far as he could see, Britain and France could be counted on to respond to his take-over of Poland in the same way they had responded to the loss of Czechoslovakia. Chamberlain's offers of concessions presented through secret contacts only confirmed Hitler's beliefs that the men of Munich would not stand up to him. It was his failing that he simply could not grasp the immense effect that the fall of Czechoslovakia and the surrender of Memel had on his foes. Finally, his decision to use force in settling old scores with the Poles prevented the British and French from deserting Beck as they had deserted Benes.

He might have achieved his aims—or at least Germany's aims—without war. He might have been able to exploit Poland economically merely by persistent negotiations. Danzig and the Polish Corridor in themselves were never worth a war to Britain and France, and they were quite prepared to let Hitler dominate southeastern Europe. But that was not enough for Hitler. A captive of his own ideology, he could not stop with economic exploitation but was determined upon a complete reversal of the Treaty of Versailles, upon domination of Europe, and upon a gathering of all Germans into a greater Reich.

It is, of course, true that Hitler had never planned the world war that developed from the Polish invasion. He had expected a short war that would be over so quickly that Britain and France would have to consider the results as a *fait accompli*. It was a gamble, but Hitler was accustomed to gambling. He had gambled before when the odds were greater, and he had won. However, in September 1939, his gambling luck ran out, and the whole world had to pay his debts.

Bibliographical Essay

The study of the origins of World War II has been hampered by the inexcusable delay in the publication of the diplomatic documents. Although it is fashionable to downgrade their importance, they are indispensable for the writing of a full scale study of the origins of World War II. As yet there is no single study on World War II that is equal in scope to the works on World War I written by Sidney B. Fay, Bernadotte Schmitt, and Luigi Albertini. Without the publication of the necessary documents twenty years after the Peace Conference, these books could never have been written. When more documents become available, then a complete study of the origins of World War II can be written.

Almost any book on European diplomacy and history during the years 1919–1939 deals in some fashion with the origins of World War II. Many of these books have become outdated following the publication of diplomatic correspondence and memoirs after the war. In this essay I have omitted most of these works, retaining only those that still have value.

For a good bibliography on the subject consult the Council on Foreign Relations, *Foreign Affairs Bibliography, 1919–1932* (New York, 1933); *1932–1942* (New York, 1945); *1942–1952* (New York, 1955); *1952–1962* (New York, 1964). Mario Toscano, *The History of Treaties and International Politics*, Pt. I: *An Introduction to the History of Treaties and International Politics: The Documentary and Memoir Sources* (Baltimore, 1966) is a masterly examination of the source materials on the diplomacy of World War I and World War II.

Good surveys of the period between the world wars include G. M. Gathorne-Hardy, *A Short History of International Affairs, 1920–1939* (London and New York, 1950); E. H. Carr, *International Relations Between the Two Wars (1919–1939)* (London, 1963); Maurice Baumont, *La faillité de la paix, 1918–1939* (2 vols., rev. ed.; Paris, 1961); P. B. Duroselle, *Histoire diplomatique de 1919 à nos jours* (Paris, 1953); and Pierre Renouvin, *War and Aftermath, 1914–1929* (New York, 1968), and his *World War II and its Origins, 1929–1945* (New York, 1969).

Royal Institute of International Affairs, *Survey of International Affairs* (London and New York, 1923–   ) provides an indispensable yearly account of events since 1920. The series was halted during the war and resumed in 1951 using the newly published diplomatic documents. Beginning with the Czechoslovak crisis, *1938*, vols. II–III (1951), *The World in March 1939* (1952), and *The Eve of the War 1939* (1958) give the best survey of the eighteen months preceding the outbreak of war.

A. J. P. Taylor, *The Origins of the Second World War* (London, 1961, and subsequent American editions) is controversial, occasionally inaccurate, but always interesting. Taylor's interpretation should be treated critically and balanced off with more orthodox accounts. Despite the criticisms of his book, Taylor has a great deal to offer. Some of the better comments on his book include G. F. Hudson, "An Apologia for Adolf Hitler," *Commentary*, XXXIII (February, 1962), 178–184; Robert Spencer, "War Unpremeditated?" *The Canadian Historical Review*, XLII (June, 1962), 136–144; and T. W. Mason, "Some Origins of the Second World War," *Past and Present*, XXIX (December, 1964), 67–87. D. C. Watt, "Appeasement: The Rise of a Revisionist School?" *Political Quarterly*, XXXVI (April, 1965), 191–213, is an important historiographical study.

On the history of the peace treaties and the postwar problems, Paul Birdsall, *Versailles Twenty Years After* (New York,

1941) is a good but now dated account of the writing of the Versailles Treaty. Ferdinand Czernin, *Versailles 1919* (New York, 1961) contains a useful collection of documents on the Paris Peace Conference and the Treaty. The best recent study is Seth P. Tillman, *Anglo-American Relations at the Paris Peace Conference of 1919* (Princeton, 1961). Arno J. Mayer, *Politics and Diplomacy of Peacemaking: Containment and Counterrevolution at Versailles, 1918–1919* (New York, 1968), is a massive study of the forces which influenced the Paris Peace Conference. For the German side, there is Alma Luckau, *The German Delegation at the Paris Peace Conference* (New York, 1941). John Maynard Keynes, *The Economic Consequences of the Peace* (New York, 1920) should be supplemented by Étienne Mantoux, *The Carthaginian Peace or the Economic Consequences of Mr. Keynes* (New York, 1952). Harold Nicolson's *Peacemaking 1919* (Boston, 1933) is a powerful indictment of the victors and their peace. Robert H. Ferrell, *Peace in Their Time: the Origin of the Kellogg-Briand Pact* (New Haven, 1952) is excellent; and Edward W. Bennett, *The Diplomacy of the Financial Crisis 1931* (Cambridge, 1962) is important. On the League of Nations the best study is F. P. Walters, *History of the League of Nations* (2 vols.; New York, 1952), and there is a sympathetic study by Byron Dexter, *The Years of Opportunity: The League of Nations, 1920–1926* (New York, 1967). On the Disarmament Conference, read John W. Wheeler-Bennett, *The Pipe Dream of Peace: The Story of the Collapse of Disarmament* (New York, 1935). For Eastern Europe, consult John A. Lukacs, *The Great Powers and Eastern Europe* (New York, 1953), and the competent survey by C. A. Macartney and A. W. Palmer, *Independent Eastern Europe* (New York, 1962). Gordon A. Craig and Felix Gilbert, *The Diplomats, 1919–1939* (2 vols.; New York, 1963) is the best work on the diplomats and their professional activities. Two books written before the documents were available are still significant: W. M. Jordan, *Great Britain, France and the German Problem 1918–1939* (London, 1943), and Arnold Wolfers, *Britain and France Between Two Wars: Conflicting Strategies of Peace Since Versailles* (New York, 1940).

For the history of Germany between the wars, S. William Halperin, *Germany Tried Democracy* (New York, 1946) is an excellent survey; in a masterful work, Erich Eyck, *A History of the Weimar Republic* (2 vols.; Cambridge, 1962–63) gives a detailed account of German political history. The problems of German diplomacy are examined in Paul Seabury, *The Wilhelmstrasse* (Berkeley, 1954). For Stresemann, see Henry L. Bretton, *Stresemann and the Revision of Versailles* (Stanford, 1953) and Hans Gatzke, *Stresemann and the Rearmament of Germany* (Baltimore, 1954). The German army and its influence on foreign policy have been examined in a number of excellent books. These include Harold J. Gordon, *The Reichswehr and the German Republic 1919–1926* (Princeton, 1957); F. L. Carsten, The *Reichswehr and Politics 1918 to 1933;* (Oxford, 1966); John W. Wheeler-Bennett, *The Nemesis of Power: The German Army in Politics, 1918–1945* (2d ed.; New York, 1964); and Robert J. O'Neill, *The German Army and the Nazi Party, 1933–1939* (London, 1966), an outstanding book.

The best introduction to Hitler is Alan Bullock's classic, *Hitler, A Study in Tyranny* (rev. ed.; New York, 1962). Hitler's speeches are in Norman H. Baynes, ed., *The Speeches of Adolf Hitler, April 1922–August 1939* (2 vols.; London, 1942). His comments and observations can be found in H. R. Trevor-Roper, ed., *Hitler's Secret Conversations, 1941–1944* (New York, 1953). For his ideas before he came to power, see *Mein Kampf* (Boston, 1943), and *Hitler's Secret Book* (New York, 1961). *Hitler*, edited by George H. Stein (Englewood Cliffs, 1968) is very useful in understanding Hitler. His early years are studied in Franz Jetzinger, *Hitler's Youth* (London, 1958). Konrad Heiden, *Der Fuehrer* (Boston, 1944) is still useful; and Hermann Rauschning, *The Voice of Destruction* (New York, 1940) is an important source for Hitler's ideas on foreign policy shortly after he came to power. William L. Shirer, *The Rise and Fall of the Third Reich* (New York, 1960) is a readable account.

John W. Wheeler-Bennett's classic, *Munich: Prologue to Tragedy* (New York, 1948) is more than a study of the September crisis. Wheeler-Bennett's knowledge of Europe makes it indispensable. Christopher Thorne, *The Approach of War, 1938–1939* (New York, 1967) is a useful synthesis. Leonard Mosley, *On Borrowed Time: How World War II Began* (New York, 1969) covers events from the Czech crisis to the outbreak of the war. Although Mosley tells an exciting story, exploiting fully his personal contacts and interviews, his interpretations are often unsound.

Gaetano Salvemini, *Prelude to World War II* (New York, 1954) stresses the role of Italy. Elizabeth Wiskemann, *The Rome–Berlin Axis: A History of the Relations between Hitler and Mussolini* (New York, 1949) is still valuable, but it should be supplemented by Ivone Kirkpatrick, *Mussolini: A Study in Power* (New York, 1964). For Mussolini's attitude towards the League of Nations before the Ethiopian crisis, see James Barros, *The Corfu Incident of 1923: Mussolini and the League of Nations* (Princeton, 1965). On the Italo-Ethiopian crisis, Royal Institute of International Affairs, *Survey of International Affairs 1935* (London, 1936) still has merit. For a detailed account of the origins of the struggle between Italy and Ethiopia, there is a first rate study by George W. Baer, *The Coming of the Italian–Ethiopian War* (Cambridge, 1967). Henderson Braddick, "The Hoare–Laval Plan: A Study in International Politics," *Review of Politics*, XXIV (July, 1962), 342–364, is essential. Brice Harris, *The United States and the Italo-Ethiopian Crisis* (Stanford, 1964) is helpful on the American view. Ferdinand Siebert offers a fresh interpretation of Italian foreign policy in *Italiens Weg in den Zweiten Weltkrieg* (Frankfurt am Main, 1962). Konrad Hugo Jarausch, *The Four Power Pact 1933* (Madison, 1965) is a thorough examination of this strange pact. Hugh Thomas, *The Spanish Civil War* (New

York, 1961) is the most comprehensive study of this conflict. A critical view of Anglo-French policy is presented in Dante A. Puzzo, *Spain and the Great Powers* (New York, 1962). The best study of the Soviet role is David T. Cattell, *Soviet Diplomacy and the Spanish Civil War* (Berkeley, 1957). Mario Toscano, *The Origins of the Pact of Steel* (Baltimore, 1967) is a classic study of this pact.

On the Austrian problem there is V. Eichstadt, *Von Dollfuss zu Hitler; Geschichte des Anschlusses Österreich, 1933–1938* (Weisbaden, 1955), an important work, and Jurgen Gehl, *Austria, Germany, and the Anschluss 1931–1938* (London, 1963). Gordon Brook-Shepherd, *Prelude to Infamy: The Story of Chancellor Dollfuss of Austria* (Cleveland, 1962) is too sentimental, but his *The Anschluss* (Philadelphia, 1963) is first rate. C. E. R. Gedye, *Fallen Bastions: The Central European Tragedy* (London, 1939) is a good journalistic account. For the effects of the July 11, 1936 Agreement, consult Keith Eubank, "Conquest by Diplomacy," *The Southwestern Social Science Quarterly, XXXIX* (June, 1958), 18–27.

Piotr Wandyczk, *France and Her Eastern Allies, 1919–1925: French–Czechoslovak–Polish Relations from the Paris Peace Conference to Locarno* (Minneapolis, 1962) is a brilliant work. Polish foreign relations can be studied in Bohdan B. Budurowycz, *Polish–Soviet Relations, 1932–1939* (New York, 1963), and Josef Korbel, *Poland Between East and West: Soviet and German Diplomacy toward Poland, 1919–1933* (Princeton, 1963). For a good survey of Polish foreign policy, there is Roman Debicki, *Foreign Policy of Poland 1919–1939: From the Rebirth of the Polish Republic to World War II* (New York, 1962). Anna M. Cienciala, *Poland and the Western Powers, 1938–1939: A Study in the Interdependence of Eastern and Western Europe* (London, 1968) is essential for an understanding of Polish foreign policy.

On German rearmament see Georges Castellan, *Le Réarmament clandestin du Reich, 1930–1935* (Paris, 1954), and Gerhard Meinck, *Hitler und die deutsche Aufrüstung, 1933–1937* (Wiesbaden, 1959). For the German economy and its relation to foreign policy, Burton H. Klein, *Germany's Economic Preparations for War* (Cambridge, 1959) is useful but should be corrected by Alan S. Milward, *The German Economy at War* (London, 1965). Sir Charles Webster and Noble Frankland, *The Strategic Air Offensive Against Germany*, vol. I (4 vols.; London, 1961) is also significant.

Boris Celovsky, *Das Münchener Abkommen von 1938* (Stuttgart, 1958) is a masterful book. Keith Eubank, *Munich* (Norman, 1963) discusses the Czechoslovak crisis and its aftermath. Laurence Thomson, *The Greatest Treason: The Untold Story of Munich* (New York, 1968) presents both new material and new interpretations. For the Sudeten German problem, there is Radomir Luza, *The Transfer of the Sudeten Germans: A Study of Czech–German Relations, 1933–1962* (New York, 1964). The lack of Czechoslovak documents has prevented study of this aspect of the Munich Agreement. Hubert Ripka, *Munich: Before and After* (London, 1939) is an adequate Czech account. Henri Noguères, *Munich* (London, 1965) gives a French view of the crisis. Interest in the Munich crisis has produced a number of excellent articles. Among these are John M. Haight Jr., "France, the United States, and the Munich Crisis," *Journal of Modern History*, XXXII (December, 1960), 340–358; J. W. Bruegel, "German Diplomacy and the Sudeten Question before 1938," *International Affairs*, XXVII (July, 1961), 323–331; and Gerhard L. Weinberg, "Secret Hitler–Benes Negotiations in 1936–37," *Journal of Central European Affairs*, XIX (January, 1960), 366–374. Interesting discussions of the May Crisis include Gerhard L. Weinberg, "The May Crisis, 1938," *Journal of Modern History*, XXIX (September, 1957), 213–225; W. V. Wallace, "The Making of the May Crisis of 1938," *Slavonic and East European Review*, XLI (June, 1963), 368–390, and D. C. Watt, "The May Crisis of 1938: A Rejoinder to Mr. Wallace," XLIV (July, 1966), 475–486. A useful collection of documents and readings on the Munich Crisis is *Peace or Appeasement? Hitler, Chamberlain, and the Munich Crisis*, edited by Francis L. Loewenheim (Boston, 1965). For a fascinating series of on-the-spot reports from Prague, consult George F. Kennan, *From Prague After Munich: Diplomatic Papers, 1938–1940* (Princeton, 1968). The best survey of British history for this period is A. J. P. Taylor, *English History 1914–1945* (New York, 1965), perhaps Taylor's best book. The finest study of British foreign policy in this era is F. S. Northedge, *The Troubled Giant: Britain Among the Great Powers, 1916–1939* (London, 1966). Martin Gilbert and Richard Gott, *The Appeasers* (Boston, 1963), an attack on appeasement policies, should be supplemented by the fine book of Derek Wood and Derek Dempster, *The Narrow Margin* (New York, 1961) which throws new light on British rearmament. Two other studies of appeasement are Margaret George, *The Warped Vision, British Foreign Policy, 1933–1939* (Pittsburgh, 1965), overly critical, and Martin Gilbert, *The Roots of Appeasement* (London, 1966) which places the problem in historical perspective. For the views of the opponents of appeasement, see William R. Rock, *Appeasement on Trial: British Foreign Policy and its Critics, 1938–1939* (Hamden, 1966). D. C. Watt, *Personalities and Politics: Studies in the Formation of British Foreign Policy in the Twentieth Century* (Notre Dame, 1965) is indispensable. For Chamberlain's pledge of March 31, 1939, see T. Desmond Williams, "Negotiations leading to the Anglo-Polish Agreement of 31 March 1939," *Irish Historical Studies*, X (1957), 59–93, 156–192, and Keith Eubank, "The British Pledge to Poland: Prelude to War," *The Southwestern Social Science Quarterly*, XLVI (March, 1965) 340–348.

Telford Taylor, *Sword and Swastika: Generals and Nazis in the Third Reich* (New York, 1952) is important. G. Gafencu, *Last Days of Europe* (New Haven, 1948) has interesting material on European diplomacy in the spring of 1939. Walther Hofer, *War Premeditated* (London, 1954) describes the final crisis during August 1939; it has been superceded by *Survey of International Affairs, The Eve of the War, 1939* (London and New York, 1958).

W. N. Medlicott, *The Coming of the War in 1939* (London, 1963) must not be overlooked. The best volume on American foreign policy is still William L. Langer and S. Everett Gleason, *The Challenge to Isolation, 1937–1940* (New York, 1952). For Hitler's views on American foreign policy, see the early chapters of James V. Compton, *The Swastika and the Eagle: Hitler, the United States, and the Origins of World War II* (Boston, 1967), a masterly treatment. For the practice of appeasement by the United States, see Arnold A. Offner, *American Appeasement: United States Foreign Policy and Germany* (Cambridge, 1969).

Arthur H. Furnia, *The Diplomacy of Appeasement: Anglo-French Relations and the Prelude to World War II, 1931–1938* (Washington, 1960) has merit but tends to be overly partial to Daladier. Esmonde M. Robertson's, *Hitler's Pre-War Policy and Military Plans, 1933–1939* (London, 1963) is enlightening. L. B. Namier, *Europe in Decay: A Study in Disintegration, 1936–1940* (New York, 1950) and *In the Nazi Era* (New York, 1952) are excellent critical analyses of documentary collections and memoirs.

A thorough study of French foreign policy for this era has not yet been written, but Alexander Werth, *The Twilight of France, 1933–1940* (New York, 1942) can still be read with profit. James Joll edited *The Decline of the Third Republic* (London, 1959) which contains important studies on the Republic in the 1930s, particularly W. F. Knapp's essay, "The Rhineland Crisis of March 1936," 67–85. The best study of the Rhineland Crisis is Jean-Baptiste Duroselle, "France and the Crisis of March 1936," *French Society and Culture since the Old Regime*, edited by Evelyn M. Acomb and Marvin L. Brown, Jr. (New York, 1964), 243–267. Donald Cameron Watt, "German Plans for the Reoccupation of the Rhineland: A Note," *Journal of Contemporary History,* I (October, 1966), 193–199, is essential to interpret the Crisis. The best treatment of the Franco-Soviet Pact is William Evans Scott, *Alliance Against Hitler: The Origins of the Franco-Soviet Pact* (Durham, 1962). Much can be learned about French foreign policy and public opinion in Charles A. Micaud, *The French Right and Nazi Germany* (Durham, 1943).

Despite the paucity of documents and memoirs from the Russians, there are a number of useful accounts. Basic studies of Soviet foreign policy are Louis Fischer, *The Soviets in World Affairs, 1917–1929* (2 vols.; Princeton, 1951); Adam B. Ulam, *Expansion and Coexistence: The History of Soviet Foreign Policy, 1917–1967* (New York, 1968); George F. Kennan, *Russia and the West Under Lenin and Stalin* (Boston, 1961); Max Beloff, *The Foreign Policy of Soviet Russia, 1929–1941* (2 vols.; London, 1947–49); Beloff's article "Soviet Foreign Policy, 1929–41: Some Notes," *Soviet Studies,* II (1950–51), 132–137; Robert D. Warth, *Soviet Russia in World Politics* (New York, 1963); *Russian Foreign Policy: Essays in Historical Perspective,* edited by Ivo J. Lederer (New Haven, 1962); and Jan Librach, *The Rise of the Soviet Empire: A Study of Soviet Foreign Policy* (New York, 1964). On Nazi–Soviet Relations, see Gerald Freund, *The Unholy Alliance: Russian–German Relations from the Treaty of Brest Litovsk to the Treaty of Berlin* (London, 1957); the classic, Gerhard Weinberg, *Germany and the Soviet Union* (Leiden, 1954); and E. H. Carr, *German–Soviet Relations Between the Two World Wars* (Baltimore, 1951). Russo-German relations before the Nazis came to power can be followed in Kurt Rosenbaum, *Community of Fate: German–Soviet Diplomatic Relations, 1922–1928* (Syracuse, 1965), and Harvey Leonard Dyck, *Weimar Germany and Soviet Russia, 1926–1933: A Study in Diplomatic Instability* (New York, 1966). Gustav Hilger and Alfred G. Meyer, *The Incompatible Allies: A Memoir–History of German–Soviet Relations, 1918–1941* (New York, 1953), is an important work by a German diplomat who served in Moscow. James E. McSherry, *Stalin, Hitler and Europe, 1933–1939: The Origins of World War II* (Cleveland, 1968) is an essential revisionist work. Some studies with insight into Soviet foreign policy are Boris I. Nicolaevsky, *Power and the Soviet Elite: The Letter of an old Bolshevik, and other Essays*

(New York, 1965); Hugh Seton-Watson, *From Lenin to Khru-schev: The History of World Communism* (New York, 1960); Franz Borkenau, *European Communism* (New York, 1953); John Erickson, *The Soviet High Command* (London, 1962); and John A. Armstrong, *The Politics of Totalitarianism: the Communist Party of the Soviet Union from 1934 to the Present* (New York, 1961).

C. A. Macartney, *October Fifteenth: A History of Modern Hungary* (2nd ed.; Edinburgh, 1961) is especially valuable on foreign policy. Also consult Stephen D. Kertesz, *Diplomacy in a Whirlpool: Hungary Between Nazi Germany and Soviet Russia,* (Notre Dame, 1953). Christoph M. Kimmich, *The Free City: Danzig and German Foreign Policy, 1919–1934* (New Haven, 1968) is a thorough analysis based on new sources. On the Danzig problem, Hans J. Leonhardt, *Nazi Conquest of Danzig* (Chicago, 1942) is still useful. Adrian Ball, *The Last Day of the Old World* (London, 1963) tells the story of September 3, 1939.

Memoirs and biographies are voluminous but they should be treated with caution. Some compensate for the lack of documents. Among the more valuable for France are Georges Bonnet, *Défense de la paix* (2 vols.; Geneva, 1946–47), which, despite the author's bias, is most important; André François-Poncet, *The Fateful Years: Memoirs of a French Ambassador in Berlin, 1931–1939* (New York, 1949), of little value since the French documents have begun to appear; Robert Coulondre, *De Staline à Hitler; souvenirs de deux ambassades, 1936–1939* (Paris, 1950); and Léon Noël, *L'Aggression Allemande contre la Pologne* (Paris, 1946). Anatole de Monzie, *Ci-devant* (Paris, 1946) and Jean Zay, *Carnets secrets de Jean Zay (de Munich à la guerre)* (Paris, 1942) are good for the attitudes of the French cabinet. J. Paul-Boncour, *Entre deux guerres, souvenirs sur la IIIe République* (3 vols.; Paris, 1945–46), and Maurice Gamelin, *Servir* (2 vols.; Paris, 1946) are both useful. For a critical view of French foreign policy, see Paul Reynaud, *In the Thick of the Fight, 1930–1945* (New York, 1955). Georges Suarez, *Briand, Sa Vie—son oeuvre, avec son journal et de nombreux documents inédits* (6 vols.; Paris, 1952) contains important documents. Alfred Mallet, *Pierre Laval* (2 vols.; Paris, 1955) has limited value, and Pierre-Étienne Flandin, *Politique française, 1919–1940* (Paris, 1947) does not tell all that he knows. Joel Colton, *Leon Blum: Humanist in Politics* (New York, 1966) is a definitive biography. Paul Stehlin, *Témoignage pour l'histoire* (Paris, 1964) is valuable for Stehlin's account of his years in Berlin as the assistant French air attache.

Among the memoirs and biographies of British statesmen and generals, Winston S. Churchill, *The Gathering Storm* (Boston, 1948) has become a classic. But had Churchill been a member of the Baldwin and Chamberlain governments, he would have written an entirely different book. *The Memoirs of Anthony Eden, Earl of Avon: Facing the Dictators* (Boston, 1962) reveals more than Eden realized. This book is essential to an understanding of much of British policy during the years 1931–1938. R. J. Minney, *Private Papers of Hore-Belisha* (London, 1960), and Alfred Duff Cooper, Viscount Norwich, *Old Men Forget* (London, 1953) contain valuable accounts of discussions in the Chamberlain cabinet. Keith Feiling, *The Life of Neville Chamberlain* (London, 1946), and Iain Macleod, *Neville Chamberlain* (London, 1961) are sympathetic studies, useful for quotations from his letters and diaries. Ramsay MacDonald awaits his biographer. For Baldwin there is G. M. Young, *Stanley Baldwin* (London, 1952); it is adequate at best. Lord Vansittart, *The Mist Procession* (London, 1958) contains some information but Vansittart's turbid style obscures his meaning. Ian Colvin, *None so Blind: A British View of the Origins of World War II* (New York, 1965), a study of Vansittart's years in the Foreign Office, is useful chiefly for quotations from his papers. A. L. Rowse, *All Souls and Appeasement* (London, 1961) is disappointing; it contains only a few interesting personal observations. Appeasement is strongly defended in Samuel Hoare, Viscount Templewood, *Nine Troubled Years* (London, 1954), and in Neville Henderson's, *Failure of a Mission: Berlin, 1937–1939* (New York, 1940) and in his *Water Under the*

Bridge (New York, 1945). Earl of Halifax, *Fullness of Days* (London, 1957) reveals very little, but Lord Birkenhead, *Halifax* (London, 1966) is a good sympathetic biography. Lord Strang, *At Home and Abroad* (London, 1956) throws light on the Czechoslovak crisis and the Moscow talks in the summer of 1939. Geoffrey Dawson and the influence of *The Times* on British foreign policy are treated in *The History of the Times: The 150th Anniversary and Beyond, 1912–1948*, Part II, *1921–1948* (London, 1952). Ivone Kirkpatrick, *The Inner Circle* (London, 1959) describes British diplomacy in Berlin. See also Tom Jones, *A Diary with Letters, 1931–50* (London, 1954), and J. R. M. Butler, *Lord Lothian* (New York, 1960) for insights into the ways of the appeasers. For the decline of British foreign policy consult Walford Selby, *Diplomatic Twilight* (London, 1953). Vincent Massey, *What's Past is Prologue* (New York, 1964) is essential for Commonwealth opinion on British foreign policy. The military problems are covered in *Time Unguarded: The Ironside Diaries, 1937–1940*, edited by Roderick Macleod and Denis Kelly (New York, 1962); *The Liddell Hart Memoirs* (2 vols.; New York, 1965–66); and Sir John Slessor, *The Central Blue: Recollections and Reflections* (London, 1956). From the Labor opposition, the best book is Hugh Dalton, *The Fateful Years: Memoirs, 1931–1945* (London, 1957). Lord D'Abernon, *An Ambassador of Peace* (3 vols.; London, 1929–1931) is an important account of his mission to Berlin, 1920–1926. Charles Petrie, *Austen Chamberlain* (2 vols.; London, 1934–40) contains letters and quotations from Chamberlain's diary. The autobiography of Simon has no value. The battle against appeasement waged by a leading Tory is told in volume III of L. S. Amery, *My Political Life* (3 vols; London, 1955). Maurice Peterson, *Both Sides of the Curtain: An Auto-biography* (London 1950) contains material on Britain and the Italo-EthiopianWar.

Among German memoirs and biographies, a basic work is *Gustav Stresemann: His Diaries, Letters and Papers* (3 vols.; New York, 1935). Here a good biography is sorely needed. Stresemann's correspondence, now available on microfilm has been studied in Hans W. Gatzke, "The Stresemann Papers," *Journal of Modern History*, XXVI (March, 1954), 49–59. Herbert von Dirksen, *Moscow, Tokyo, London: Twenty Years of German Foreign Policy* (Norman, 1952) has limited value. Personalities and the atmosphere of the pre-war negotiations can be found in Paul Schmidt, *Hitler's Interpreter* (New York, 1951). Ernst von Weizsaecker, *Memoirs* (Chicago, 1951) is a weak apologia. An interesting account of the German Foreign Ministry can be found in Erich Kordt, *Nicht aus den Akten. Die Wilhelmstrasse in Frieden und Krieg. Erlebnisse, Begegnungen und Eindrucke 1928–1945* (Stuttgart, 1950). Franz von Papen, *Memoirs* (London, 1952) provides some significant information on Austro-German relations. *The Von Hassell Diaries, 1938–44* (London, 1948) tell the story of a diplomat who opposed Hitler.

Birger Dahlerus, *The Last Attempt* (London, 1948) is the story of his efforts as an intermediary between London and Berlin. Friedrich Hossbach, *Zwischen Wehrmacht und Hitler* (Hanover, 1949) has some importance.

Eduard Benes wrote a survey of the Munich crisis, *Memoirs: From Munich to New War and Victory* (Boston, 1954); it is not significant. His more detailed account of the Munich Crisis has never been translated into English, but there is an excellent critical summary in Otakar Odlozilik, "Eduard Benes on Munich Days," *Journal of Central European Affairs*, XVI (January, 1957), 384–393, and his "Concerning Munich and the Ides of March," *Journal of Central European Affairs*, IX (January, 1950), 419–428. Benes' ideas and policies have also been studied by his private secretary, Edward Taborsky in "The Triumph and Disaster of Eduard Benes," *Foreign Affairs*, XXXVI (July, 1958), 669–684, and "Benes and the Soviets," *Foreign Affairs*, XXVII (January, 1949), 302–314. For the Polish story there are Jozef Beck, *Final Report* (New York, 1957); *Papers and Memoirs of Jozef Lipski, Ambassador of Poland: Diplomat in Berlin, 1933–1939*, edited by Waclaw Jedrzejewicz (New York, 1968); and the diary of the

Polish Undersecretary for Foreign Affairs, Jan Szembek, *Journal 1933–1939* (Paris, 1952). Kurt von Schuschnigg has told the story of the *Anschluss* in *Austrian Requiem* (London, 1947). On Italian foreign policy read Ciano's *Hidden Diary, 1937–1938* (New York, 1953); *The Ciano Diaries, 1939–1943* (New York, 1946); and *Ciano's Diplomatic Papers* (London, 1948). There is important material on Mussolini's quarrels with the League of Nations in Pompeo Aloisi, *Journal (25 juillet 1932–14 juin 1936)* (Paris, 1957). Raffaele Guariglia, *Ricordi* (Naples, 1950) is valuable for information on Italian foreign policy, 1922–38. There is material on German–Italian relations in Massimo Magistrati, *L'Italia a Berlino (1937–1939)* (Milan, 1956). Details on Franco-Italian relations can be found in Hubert Lagardelle, *Mission à Rome: Mussolini* (Paris, 1955).

Publication of documentary collections has been far too slow. Although it has been superceded by official publications, *Trial of the Major War Criminals before the International Military Tribunal, Proceedings and Documents* (42 vols.; Nuremberg, 1947–49) is still unique. Many of the documents collected for the trial have been published in *Nazi Conspiracy and Aggression* (10 vols.; Washington, D. C., 1946–48). There is some useful material on German foreign policy in the trials of the minor war criminals: *Trials of the War Criminals before the Nuremberg Military Tribunals under Control Council Law N. 10* (15 vols.; Washington, D. C., n.d.). The archives of the German foreign ministry captured in the closing days of the war are being published jointly by the British, American, and French governments in *Documents on German Foreign Policy 1918–1945 from the Archives of the German Foreign Ministry* (Washington, D. C., 1949–). Because of the cost of publishing so large a collection, only documents for the period 1933–1941 will appear in English. Documents for the years 1925–1933 have begun to appear in the series, *Akten zur Deutschen Auswärtigen Politik, 1918–1945, aus dem Archiv des Auswärtigen Amts* (Göttingen, 1966–). Documents on Soviet–German relations are available in *Nazi–Soviet Relations,*

1939–1941: Documents from the Archives of the German Foreign Office (Washington, D. C., 1948). *La politique allemande (1936–1943): Documents secrets du Ministère des Affaires Étrangères d'Allemande* (3 vols.; Paris, 1946–47), published by the Soviet government, contains captured German documents relating to Turkey, Hungary, and Spain. The Soviet government published German documents dealing with Anglo-German affairs in *Documents and Materials relating to the Eve of the Second World War* (2 vols.; Moscow, 1948); the second volume includes private papers of Herbert von Dirksen. Microfilmed materials from the German Foreign Ministry archives have been catalogued in *A Catalogue of German Foreign Ministry Files and Microfilms 1867–1920* (Oxford, 1959), and *A Catalog of Files and Microfilms of the German Foreign Ministry Archives, 1920–1945,* edited by George Kent (Stanford, 1962). Microfilmed documents available for purchase from The National Archives are listed in *Index of Microfilmed Records of the German Foreign Ministry and the Reich's Chancellery covering the Weimar Period* (Washington, D. C., 1958).

The British government is publishing a collection *Documents on British Foreign Policy* 1919–1939 (London, 1947–). The third series, covering events from the *Anschluss* to the outbreak of the war, has been completed. At the moment this is the most significant documentary source in print for the study of this period. The wealth of material presented and the role of Britain in the diplomacy of the period make it essential. The British archives are now open to 30 years from the current year.

Because much of the correspondence from the Foreign Ministry archives was destroyed in 1940, French documents have only recently begun to be published in *Documents diplomatiques français 1932–1939* (Paris, 1964–). The record of a parliamentary investigation of the origins of the war and the defeat of France was published in *Les événements survenus en France de 1933 à 1945. Temoignagnes et documents recueillis par la commission d'enquete parlementaire* (11 vols.; Paris, 1947–51). Although it contains some important documents, it should be used with caution. A wartime publication which still has value is *The French Yellow Book: Diplomatic Documents, 1938–1939* (New York, 1940).

Foreign Relations of the United States: Diplomatic Papers, published annually, has a unique value becaue it is the only collection now available for the entire post-1919 period. In addition, as a part of this series, the United States government has published 13 volumes on the Paris Peace Conference of 1919—the only major power to do so. State Department files in the National Archives are open to 30 years from the current year. Beyond that date, access by American scholars to the documents is restricted to those years which have been covered in the published volumes of *Foreign Relations of the United States.*

The Italian government is publishing a voluminous collection of source materials covering Italian foreign policy, 1861–1943, *I Documenti Diplomatici Italiani* (Rome, 1952–   ), in nine series. Series six, seven, and eight are pertinent to the study of the origins of World War II. Belgian documents are available in *Documents diplomatiques belges 1920–1940* (Brussels, 1964–   ). Hungary is the first Communist government to begin systematic publication of documents on pre-war diplomacy in *Diplomáciai iratok Magyaroszág Külpolitikájához 1936–1945* [Hungarian Foreign Policy Documents, 1936–1945] (Budapest, 1962–   ). There is also a series on Portuguese diplomacy, *Dez anos de política externa (1936–1947). A Nação portugesa e a segunda guerra mundial* (Libson, 1961–   ).

The only Polish documents available are in a Polish White Book published at the outbreak of war, *Official Documents concerning Polish–German and Polish–Soviet Relations, 1933–1939* (New York, 1940). Only a few Czechoslovak documents arc available in *Europäische Politik 1933–1938, im Spiegel der Prager Akten,* edited by Friedrich Berber (Essen, 1942), which contains documents captured by the Germans, and in a thin selection by the Ministry for Foreign Affairs of the Czechoslovak Republic,

New Documents on the History of Munich (Prague, 1958). For a commentary on the Czechoslovak publication consult, William W. Wallace, "New Documents on the History of Munich," *International Affairs,* XXXV (October, 1959), 447–454. There are no documents yet in print from the Soviet archives although they have been promised. *Soviet Documents on Foreign Policy,* edited by Jane Degras (3 vols.; London, 1951–53) contains public speeches and Soviet diplomatic correspondence which have been published in other collections. A very useful compilation of speeches and published diplomatic correspondence can be found in the volumes of the Royal Institute of International Affairs, *Documents on International Affairs* (London, 1929–).

Specialized studies on topics in European diplomacy for the years 1919–1939 continue to appear. Anyone interested in current publications should consult *The Journal of Modern History, The American Historical Review, International Affairs* (London), *Foreign Affairs, Vierteljahrshefte für Zeitgeschichte,* and *La Revue de l'histoire de la deuxième guerre mondiale.*

Index

Adowa, 48
Alexander, King of Yugoslavia, 41
Allied Control Commission, 5, 22, 32
Anglo-American Treaties of Guarantee, 10
Anglo-German Declaration, 116–117
Anglo-German Naval Agreement, 43–45, 116
Anglo-Polish Alliance, 160
Anschluss, 35, 86–98, 168
appeasement, 9, 33, 73–80, 120, 123, 128–129, 165, 167–168
Arciszewski, Miroslaw, 142
armistice, 1–3
Astakov, Georgei, 150, 153
Australia, 48
Austria, 82
    and *Anschluss*, 86–98, 168
Austro-German Agreement, 88–90
Austro-German Customs Union, 86–87

Baldwin, Stanley, 44, 74–75, 78
    on Hoare–Laval Pact, 53–55
    and Rhineland. 60, 64–65
Barthou, Louis, 40–41
Beck, Jozef
    and British pledge, 139–140
    career of, 130–131
    in Czechoslovak crisis, 112, 122, 131–132
    and Danzig, 132–134, 138
    foreign policy of, 131–132, 136–137, 141–142
    in Polish crisis, 162
Beck, General Ludwig, 105, 114
Belgium, 17, 66
Benes, Eduard, 101, 106–107, 109, 117, 134
Beran, Rudolf, 127
Berchtesgaden
    Hitler–Chamberlain conference, 108–109
    Hitler–Schuschnigg conference, 91–93
Bismarck, Otto von, 6
Blitzkrieg warfare, 38–39
Blomberg, Marshal Werner von, 32, 62
    directive of December 7, 84
    marriage of, 85
    in Reichschancellery meeting, 81, 83–84
Blum, Leon, 71–72
Bonar Law, Andrew, 78
Bonnet, Georges, 102–104, 109, 111, 125
    on Franco-German declaration, 123–124

Bonnet, Georges (cont.)
  on occupation of Czechoslovakia,
    128
Brauchitsch, General Walther von,
    85, 105, 138
Brest-Litovsk, Treaty of, 6, 12
Bruening, Heinrich, 32
Bulgaria, 19
Bullitt, William, 131

Canada, 128
Chamberlain, Joseph, 75
Chamberlain, Neville
  aggreement with Hitler, 116–117
  and appeasement, 78–79, 123,
    128–129, 165
  conferences with Daladier and
    Bonnet, 109, 111
  conference with Hitler at Berch-
    tesgaden, 108–109
  conference with Hitler at Godes-
    berg, 100
  and Czechoslovak crisis, 101–103,
    106–108
  foreign policy, 76, 141, 144
  and four-power declaration, 136–
    137
  and guarantee of Czechoslovakia,
    124–125
  in Munich Conference, 115, 117–
    118
  negotiates over Poland, 157–164
  negotiates with U.S.S.R., 149–150,
    152
  on occupation of Czechoslovakia,
    128–129
  personality of, 75
  pledge to Poland, 139–140
  quarrel with Eden, 76–77
  seeks arrangement with Hitler,
    144–145
Chvalkovsy, Frantisek, 127
Ciano, Count Galeazzo, 47, 122, 133
  conference with Hitler, 154–155
Clemenceau, Georges, 4, 10, 86
Colvin, Ian, 139

Corfu, occupation of, 14–15
Council of Four, 4
Coulondre, Robert, 159
Czechoslovakia, 17, 82
  Hungary and, 121–122
  and Munich Agreement, 116–117,
    120–121
  occupation of, 128–129
  and Slovaks, 125–126
  Sudeten crisis, 98–115

Dahlerus, Birger, 160–161, 164
Daladier, Edouard, 102, 108, 113–
    114, 125, 144
  conferences with Chamberlain,
    103, 109, 111
  correspondence with Hitler, 159,
    161
  at Munich Conference, 115–117
Danzig, 5–6, 132–134, 137–139,
    142–143
Dawes Plan, 9, 23, 74
De Gaulle, Charles, 59
depression, 23–24
Dimitrov, Georgi, 67
Dollfuss, Engelbert, 35–36
Duff Cooper, Alfred, 109

Economic Consequences of the
    Peace, 11
Eden, Anthony, 37–38, 43
  Mussolini and, 51–53
  quarrel with Chamberlain, 76–77
  and Rhineland, 60, 64–65
Eastern Locarno Pact, 40–41
Ethiopia
  Mussolini and, 46, 48–51
  war with Italy, 52–53, 55

Flandin, Pierre, 58, 65–66
Four-Power Pact, 34–35
France
  alliance system, 17–19
  and Czechoslovakia, 18–19
  disarmament plan, 33–34
  pact with U.S.S.R., 39–43, 57

France (cont.)
and Poland, 16
Rhineland and, 57–60, 63–66
security of, 9–10, 66–67
Spanish Civil War and, 70–73
Treaty of Locarno and, 21–22
Franco, General Francisco, 68, 72
Franco-German declaration, 123–124
Franco-Russian Pact, 39–43, 57
François-Poncet, André, 57, 123
Frederick the Great, 109
Fritsch, General Werner von, 81, 84–85

Gamelin, General Maurice, 58–59
Geneva Disarmament Conference, 32–34
Germany
Anglo-German Naval Agreement, 43–45, 116
armistice, and 1–3
army of, 5, 12
and depression, 24
and inflation, 8–9
Treaty of Locarno and, 21–22
non-aggression pact with Poland, 40, 142
and rearmament, 37–38
trade agreement with U.S.S.R., 156
Treaty of Versailles and, 6, 11–12
Weimar Republic, 3, 6, 167
Glaise-Horstenau, Edmund, 89
Gleiwitz incident, 165
Godesberg conference, 110
Goering, Hermann, 47, 77, 81, 95, 97, 105, 127, 160, 164
Great Britain
Anglo-German Naval Agreement, 43–45, 116
and Ethiopia, 50–51, 55
negotiations with U.S.S.R., 147–152
pledge to Poland, 139–140
and Polish alliance, 160

Great Britain (cont.)
Rhineland and, 60, 64–66
Spanish Civil War and, 70, 72–73
Treaty of Locarno and, 22
Grey, Sir Edward, 141
Gruhn, Erna, 85

Hacha, Emil, 127–128, 134, 162–163
Haile Selassie, 48, 53–54
Halifax (Lord) Edward, third viscount, 103, 106, 109, 111, 122, 125, 129, 135–136, 139–141
conversation with Hitler, 77–78
personality of, 76–77
pledge to Poland, 139–141
Henderson, Neville, 158–160, 162–164
Henlein, Konrad, 99–101, 103–104, 108
Himmler, Heinrich, 85
Hitler, Adolf, 24, 34, 56
Anglo-German Naval Agreement and, 44–45, 142
Anschluss and, 87–90, 93–95, 97–98
August 14 conference, 155
August 22 conference, 157
and Jozef Beck, 131–132, 133–134
Blitzkrieg and, 38–39
conference with Chamberlain at Berchtesgaden, 108–109
conference with Chamberlain at Godesberg, 110
conference with Ciano, 154–155
conference with Schuschnigg, 91–93
conversation with Halifax, 77–78
correspondence with Chamberlain, 111–112
correspondence with Daladier, 159, 161
Czechoslovakia and, 100, 104–108, 111–115
Danzig and, 133, 137–138, 142

Hitler, Adolf (cont.)
   Dollfuss and, 35–36
   early career, 25–28
   economic planning, 39
   February 28 speech, 36–37
   on Franco-Russian Pact, 42–43
   Geneva Disarmament Conference
      and, 32–34
   on guarantee of Czechoslovakia,
      125
   and Hacha, 127–128
   January 22 speech, 85
   on Lebensraum, 22, 31, 36–37,
      105
   May 23 conference, 143–144
   and Munich Conference, 55, 115–
      117
   and Mussolini, 47, 159–160
   negotiates with Chamberlain,
      157–164
   and non-aggression pact with
      Poland, 35, 142
   occupation of Czechoslovakia and,
      124
   orders attack on Poland, 157, 160,
      164
   and rearmament, 30–32
   in Reichschancellery meeting, 81–
      84
   responsibility for war, 166, 168–
      169
   Rhineland occupation and, 56–57,
      60–63, 65–66
   September 12 broadcast, 107–108
   Spanish Civil War and, 68, 72
   and Stalin, 28–29
   tactics of, 29–30
Hoare, Sir Samuel, 52–54, 76
Hoare–Laval Pact, 53–55
Hossbach, Colonel Friedrich, 81, 83
Hungary, 19
   Czechoslovakia and, 122
   occupation of Ruthenia, 126

Italian–Ethiopian War, 46, 52–53,
   55

Italian-Ethiopian War (cont.)
   pre-war negotiations, 49–52
   Walwal incident, 48
   Italy, 19

Japan
   Manchurian crisis, 15–16

Karlsbad Demands, 100–101, 107
Keitel, General Wilhelm von, 92, 94,
   105–106
Kellogg–Briand Pact, 22–23
Kennard, Sir Howard, 162
Keynes, John Maynard, 11
Kreditanstalt, 23, 87

Laval, Pierre, 38, 41, 50, 52
   agreement with Mussolini, 49, 51
   and Hoare–Laval Pact, 53–54
League of Nations, 4
   Covenant of, 13
   and Ethiopia, 48–49, 51–56
   and Manchuria, 15–16
   and occupation of Corfu, 14–15
   and Poland, 130
   Rhineland and, 65–66
   and United States, 16
Lipski, Jozef, 132–133, 137–138,
   162, 165
Lithuania, 137
Little Entente, 17
Litvinov, Maxim, 40, 68, 112, 119,
   136
   dismissed, 148
   negotiates with British and
      French, 147, 152
Lloyd George, David, 4–5, 7, 10, 78
Locarno, Treaty of, 20–21, 75
   and Rhineland, 57–58, 61, 63, 66
Ludendorff, General Erich, 86
Lytton Commission, 15

MacDonald, J. Ramsay, 15, 43, 74,
   78
   disarmament plan, 33
   at Stresa, 38, 50

Maffey Report, 50–51
Maginot Line, 19–20, 59–60
Manchurian Crisis, 15–16
Marin, General Louis, 58
Masaryk, Thomas, 101
May Crisis, 103–104
Mein Kampf, 27, 30, 35, 87
Memel, 137–138
Merekalov, Alexei, 146–147
Miklas, Wilhelm, 95, 97
Molkte, Hans-Adolf von, 142
Molotov, V. M.
    negotiates with British and French, 148–152
    negotiates with Germans, 155–156
Munich Beer Hall *Putsch*, 27
Munich Agreement, 116–117, 120–121, 142
    guarantee of Czechoslovakia, 125
Munich Conference, 55, 115–117
Mussolini, Benito, 38, 113, 125, 154
    Anschluss and, 93–95
    early career and personality of, 46–47
    Ethiopia and, 47–56, 77
    foreign policy of, 47–48
    Four-Power Pact and, 34
    Hitler and, 60, 159–160
    in Munich Conference, 113–114
    and occupation of Corfu, 14–15
    Spanish Civil War and, 68–69

Nazi–Soviet Pact
    negotiations, 153–156
    terms of, 156
Neurath, Constantine von, 62, 81, 83–85, 105
Neustaedter-Stuermer, Odo, 89
New Zealand, 118
Nuremberg war crimes trials, 61, 157

Operation Green, 84, 104–106, 110
Operation White, 141, 164
Orlando, Vittorio, 4

Pact of Steel, 142–143
Papen, Franz von, 32, 87, 89–92
Paris Peace Conference, 3–4, 99, 116
Paul-Boncour, Joseph, 40
"Peace Ballot," 51
Petain, Marshal Henri-Philippe, 59
Philip, Prince of Hesse, 94
Poland, 130
    Danzig, 5–6, 132–134, 137–139, 142
    and France, 17–18
    minorities, 17–18
    non-aggression pact with Germany, 35, 40
    Teschen, 18–19, 122, 132
    war with Germany, 143, 164–165
Polish Corridor, 5, 12
Polish–German Non-aggression Pact, 35, 40
Popular Front, 67–68, 70–71

Raeder, Admiral Eric, 81, 105
Reichschancellery meeting, 78, 81–84, 89
reparations, 6–9
Rhineland, 6–7, 21–22
    remilitarization of, 56–69
Ribbentrop, Joachim von, 43, 91–92, 100, 105, 121–122, 126–127
    August 30 demands, 163–164
    Danzig and, 132, 134, 137–138
    Franco-German declaration and, 123–124
    negotiates Nazi–Soviet Pact, 153, 155–156
Roosevelt, Franklin D., 24, 76–77, 112
Ruhr occupation, 8–9, 74
Rumania, 17, 19, 136–137, 144
    economic agreement with Germany, 135
Runciman, Walter, 106–107
Russia, *see* Union of Soviet Socialist Republics
Ruthenia, 126

S. A., 36–37
Saar, 6, 37
Sarraut, Albert, 58–59
Scheidemann, Philipp, 3
Schmidt, Guido, 91
Schnurre, Karl, 150
Schuschnigg, Kurt von, 87–90, 134, 162–163
  and *Anschluss*, 93–96
  conference with Hitler, 91–93
Seeckt, General Hans von, 31–32
Seeds, William, 147, 149
Seyss-Inquart, Arthur, 89, 92–93, 95–97
Sidor, Karol, 126
Simon, Sir John, 37–38, 43, 76, 111
  Ethiopia and, 49–50
Slovakia, 125–126, 137
South Africa, 118
Spanish Civil War, 68–73
Stalin, Joseph V.
  Anglo-French negotiations and, 148, 150
  Franco-Russian Pact and, 42
  March 10 speech, 145–146
  Munich Agreement and, 118–119
  Nazi–Soviet Pact and, 155–156
  and nazism, 28–29
  Popular Front and, 68
  Spanish Civil War and, 69–70, 72
Strang, William, 149
Stresa Front, 38, 44, 50
Stresemann, Gustav, 20–22
Sudeten Germans, 18, 98–102, 104, 106–108, 121
Sudetenland, 99–101, 108, 113, 115–116, 118

Teschen, 18–19, 112, 122, 132

Tilea, Viorel, 135–136
Tiso, Joseph, 125–126

Union of Soviet Socialist Republics, 19
  Anglo-French negotiations and, 147–152
  and Germany, 145–146
  Munich Conference and, 118–119
  pact with France, 39–43, 57
  trade agreement with Germany, 156
United States
  League of Nations and, 16
  Senate, 10

Vansittart, Robert, 50–51, 54
Versailles, Treaty of, 3–5, 34, 44–45, 73–74, 84, 86, 167
  Article 231, 6
  Article 80, 86
  criticism of, 7, 10–12
  reparations, 7–9
  terms of, 5–6
Victor Emmanuel III, 46
Vietnam, 67
Voroshilov, Kliment E., 151–152

Walwal, 48
Weimar Republic, 3, 6, 167
  rearmament, 31–32
Weizsaecker, Ernst von, 146–147
Wilhelm II, 3, 44
Wilson, Horace, 76, 111, 145, 153
Wilson, Woodrow, 4–7, 10, 13–14, 78
Wohltat, Helmut, 135, 153

Yugoslavia, 17, 19